The ENGLISH IN LOVE

Passion Among The Elite

The
ENGLISH IN LOVE

Passion Among The Elite

Anne de Courcy

SALEM HOUSE PUBLISHERS
TOPSFIELD, MASSACHUSETTS

First published in the United States by
Salem House Publishers, 1987
462 Boston Street, Topsfield, MA 01983

Published in the United Kingdom by
Ebury Press

Library of Congress Catalog Card Number
86-62174

ISBN 0 88162 267 2

Designed by Harry Green
Illustrations by Mark Haddon
Picture research by Jenny de Gex

Computerset in Great Britain by ECM, London
Printed in Great Britain at the
University Press, Cambridge.

ACKNOWLEDGEMENTS

Among the many people who have been kind enough to help
me with advice, comment, information or insight during the
writing of this book, I would particularly like to thank the
following: Elizabeth Adams, Suzie Adam, Andrew Barber, Sally
Berner, Carole Blake, Jane and Michael Clayton, Julian Critchley
MP, James Cronin, Dr David Delvin, Robin and Tui Esser,
Lady Falkender, Julian Friedmann, David Hagan, Gillian
Haslam, Stan Hey, Adam Jacot de Boinod, Anthony Jay, Clive
Limpkin, Carol Lutostanski, Rose-Ellen Mates, Kevin Memery,
Caroline Michel, Diana Moran, Sarah Morris, Tony Morris,
Trudi Pacter, Nick Palliser, Mungo Parke, Anton Powell, Libby
Purves, Alistair Scott, Anna Scott, Peter Snape MP, Laurie
Taylor, Phil Vernon, Rosi Wilson. I owe special gratitude and
thanks to my editor, Suzanne Webber.

Contents

Introduction

The one thing to be said with certainty about falling in love is that it occupies a place in our lives important out of all proportion to the amount of time spent actively doing something about it – look at the hours of obsessive thinking, scheming and brooding that can lead up to even a simple two-minute telephone call. Otherwise, despite the inexhaustible flow of words inspired by this all-consuming emotion, defining exactly what love is and why two people are drawn irresistibly together is about as profitable as attempting to draw Leviathan up with a hook. Nothing, says the poet, is more mysterious than the way of a man with a maid.

In general, that is. But when it comes to the particular, there are exceptions. Certain worlds are so tightly enclosed within their self-imposed boundaries, so hedged about with custom, taboo or limitation and thus so circumscribed as to probabilities, that the time, the place and even the loved one are all netted in a light gauze of predictability. In other words, once you know your parameters, checking out the paramours becomes relatively easy.

'Gentlemen', said Douglas Sutherland, writing of the tribe he knows best, 'aren't basically passionate – but they do need a little bit of comfort.' He was, of course, writing of the full-time gentleman, now a sadly dwindling breed; fortunately, however, English society is full of such tightly-knit, ritualistic circles, each with an equally idiosyncratic approach to Love. In the following pages I have tried to offer a few insights into some of these.

It only remains to add that every generalisation, however sweeping – let alone all specific incidents – are based upon the direct personal observation either of myself or of a team of highly-paid and exceptionally trustworthy moles.

1 Early Stirrings

A dolescence is when you discover what a comb is for, rip off name tapes but stick on initials, find that an older brother or younger sister can provide the Open Sesame to a whole new world – and run headlong and unprepared into the joys and traumas of First Love. All of them are increased a thousandfold by a pressure normally unknown to the adult love affair: every faltering step into this unknown land is in front of a crowd of fascinated onlookers, uninhibited by restraints of taste, manners or delicacy from the dissection of every detail – an exquisite torture that from the victim's point of view is comparable only to advancing into the arena under the merciless gaze of the Roman crowd to meet some unpredictable wild animal. Along with this goes the self-consciousness of adolescence: a girl rejects a boy with a gust of giggles that makes him want to hide for a week, a boy switches to a girl's best friend in front of all her classmates at the party.

Yes, the keynote of adolescent love is lack of privacy. Even when the telephone rings (quite likely in the drawing room, in front of the rest of the family), the best friend of the one ringing up is listening in on the extension. But lack of privacy works both ways: not for nothing is one of the great teenage fantasies carrying off the most desirable boy or girl in the school *in front of everyone else*. Often, the most important thing about a first romance is that you are seen to be having one.

'My friend says she fancies you'

One essential to the first brushes between the sexes is the go-between, or more accurately, the third (and often fourth, fifth, sixth and seventh) party, not so much to pass notes or messages but to act as forward lookout post and general sounding board,

passing on items of gossip ('Simon says Mark really really likes you'). For since both parties are terrified of putting their cards on the table in case of public humiliation, hints as to whether advances are likely to be accepted or rejected are invaluable. Even while the welcome news that 'everyone' says Jane or John is passionate about you is duly being rubbished, there is the comforting knowledge that all gossip originates from somewhere. In teenage love, there is usually no fire without some smoke.

'This man keeps ringing me up and he's *rerlly* rerlly old, about 25, and I think he's quite keen on me and I'm *rerlly* rerlly embarrassed about it. If you ring me tomorrow I'll tell you all about it.'

DOING IT FOR THE CROWD

In mannered love, and perhaps in the first five minutes of
passionate love, a woman taking a lover will be more concerned with the
way other women see him than with the way she sees him herself.

STENDHAL,
De l'amour

Crashing the puberty barrier

All the way through the teens, girls are two
or three years ahead physically and light
years further on in terms of sophistication,
so for boys speed of maturation is a crucial
element. Every prep school chorister wants
to fling off his cassock as soon as he arrives
at public school, not because he has suddenly taken against music but because it's a
highly visible sign his voice hasn't broken.

Just as important is growing body hair:
this is the age of sticking on a plaster and
saying, 'I cut myself shaving' or letting the
incipient beard grow for two days and then
remarking 'I forgot to shave this morning'.
Discussions on the subject are endless: How
often? Where? Does shaving after every
meal encourage growth? Is a lot of stubble
really a sign of virility? Along with this
comes anything else that gives the necessary
reassurance of sexual identity, from after-
shave to pornography – it comes as a shock
to many boys to find that women do not
have staples through their stomachs – the
giving of marks out of ten to every passing
female, complicated code words to signal to
initiates where you got to on last night's
date, discussions whose length is in directly
opposite ratio to the amount of action
involved.

For the adolescent boy the whole pressure is on growing up, wising up, getting
there – around 15 is not only puberty time
and O-level time, it's also time for privileges
like working in your own room or varying
the school uniform or bedtime – 'You're not

allowed to act your youth. It's one big
"Haven't you done this yet? It's time you did
it" when probably you'd rather be playing
with your Lego than with girls,' says one
boy. One reason is that everyone takes as
sexual measuring-post the one or two over-
developed figures found in every class ('In
the first year, when you're all running
around in the shower room with your little
bony knees and white singlets, they're com-
bing the hairs of their chests into a side
parting') or senior boys with blue chins who
roll their own cigarettes and are reputed to
go out with nurses.

The turn-off vest

Though most girls are into thigh boots
before a boy's voice is fully broken, some are
equally late developers – one of the worst
shocks for a growing boy is to find on an
early romantic encounter that his date is
wearing a vest rather than a bra – though
anything from padding to make-up can dis-

guise this. Some girls turn to cosmetics
because of the great female worry, blushing,
often coming in to school with one side of
their face more rouged than the other
because they haven't taken the light from a
side window into account.

Rebel, rebel

Boys also forget that if a girl stays out later than the curfew set for her it isn't necessarily because of their own overweening charm but rather a desire to challenge parental restraints. Thus many of the boys who have the greatest success with adolescent girls are the teenage James Deans who lure girls into situations where rebellion is mingled inextricably with sex.

Spots

Blight of the teenage boy's life, spots cause many a promising romance to founder, let alone cripple social converse. 'You can feel one erupting a week before you have your most important date. Then you go out and you can feel it throbbing at the end of your nose, heat emanating from it until you feel everyone must be looking. When you see a boy burying his head in his hands before the disco lights come up or saying "Must get out before the last song" you know instantly why.' Even those whose spots are barely perceptible resent them bitterly as insignia

---

'It was looks all the time.
The goodlooking boys got the girls,
always, and there was nothing
you could do about it.'

---

of their lack of adulthood: spots are the equivalent of walking round with a sign saying, 'I'm not grown up yet'. Once again, girls do better: not only do they have fewer spots, what they do have can generally be disguised by make-up.

The meeting place

In the holidays the favoured spots are the coffee bar, pub, Pony Club, each other's houses, skating rink, cinema, concert, et al. With regular meeting spots, the voluntary or involuntary host should note one peculiarity: rather as many species of wild ani-

Braless in Eton

Speech days of all kinds make marvellous invitations for boys who wish to impress a particular girl. But nothing beats the Fourth of June for a setting both glamorous and romantic – the chestnut blossom like pink and white confetti, the ancient buildings, cricket on Agar's Plough, champagne in tumblers, windswept silk dresses, little girls in blue Liberty-print dresses, and everywhere the characteristic shambling slouch of the adolescent Etonian. So successful was this wonderful summer occasion as a festal outing, with hordes of recent O.E.'s turning up on their Yamahas, braless girlfriends in brief leather minis on the pillion, empty champagne bottles everywhere and couples lying entwined in the long grass by the river that, alas, the authorities have taken the only step that could prevent the mass descent on the College of its newly-employed alumni. Instead of, as formerly, on a Saturday, the Fourth of June is now held *on the fourth of June.*

Floreat Etona.

mals 'mark' a particular tree, termite mound or rock that forms a regular visiting point in their territory, so teenagers (particularly the males) 'mark' anywhere they visit frequently with their own personal insignia of carved initials, tabs of chewing gum, biro scrawls, etc.

In termtime, day school meetings go on as above, with the difference that comparing homework makes an all-purpose, all-weather opening gambit; at boarding schools much depends on the distance of the school from the nearest town/school of the opposite sex, schools in the remoter folds of Yorkshire or in the bracing air of the South Downs having a visibly lower sophistication level.

At London public schools like Harrow or Westminster where weekly boarding is the norm, senior boys sneak out at night to meet girls for clubs, balls or concerts, creeping through the kitchens after the patrolling housemaster has gone to sleep; or try to crash parties at stylish girls' schools like St Paul's or the Francis Holland. Less exotically, they coax girls into pubs, where they ply them with drink in the hope of getting them drunk – not too difficult, since teenagers choose drinks like vodka and orange, vodka and lime or bacardi and coke because these are the ones they know the

names of – not so much for instant seduction as to loosen tension and provide a shared background of illicit complicity from which an invitation to movies or warehouse party seems but natural and inevitable.

Girls in the sixth!

The most exciting time in public schools which take in girls for A-levels is the summer holidays before joining the Sixth Form. On the first day of the first Sixth Form term, in the first class with *girls* in it, teachers can make no headway for the ogling, whispering, assessing and general buzz of churning hormones. Almost immediately, there is common agreement on who are the two or three top girls, with anyone notably beautiful idolised by the whole school, especially the little boys. Older ones quickly establish themselves as leg, bum or tit men – those who pride themselves on being cool like a girl to be tall as well – but a large bust isn't always the advantage it is in later life: though fancied, the big-busted girl is often left alone because no boy wants his friends to scoff 'God, he's such a *fetishist* . . .' Insults between a girl and boy, on the other hand, are often the sign of a budding relationship.

In the more sophisticated Sixth Forms, most school relationships go the whole way, with boys who have never been in contact with girls before falling heavily in love. Most are reasonably discreet; very seldom are people so overcome by passion they do as a couple at one London public school did: leave the curtains open. Unfortunately, it was mid-morning – and the bedroom concerned was right under the Headmaster's window . . .

The mockers

Along with the other limitations – parental curfews, lack of money, no wheels so no mobility – young love has another difficulty

Pitstop at the School Dance.

which most people remember afterwards with a shudder: constant mockery or ribbing from friends and juniors. Confidence is essential even while the cheeks are red: the boy who chats up a girl while his friends are nudging each other has to assure her that they really are pathetic, aren't they? Both sides have to be prepared for the pursuers who trail courting couples to favourite venues like the nearest park, sneaking up at crucial moments, or school juniors who spot a senior and a sixth form girl having coffee and rush back to inform their friends, who then storm the cafe in a noisy troop.

Much harder to take is the pressure from jealous friends. Girls taunt each other with how wet or ugly the boy friend is ('God, he's revolting! How *can* you fancy him?'), boys get off with each others' girl friends in drunken moments at parties; but what really breaks things up is the endless, constant chipping away, with its parrot cry of 'oh-h-h, they're in *love!* How *boring* .. !', which has rung the death knell of many a teenage romance.

The school hop

School dances all run to the same basic format of boys and girls between 15 and 18 coming together for a frenzied evening's mingling that staff believe is held within the bounds of decency only by their token presence. Fortunately, this is the age where much of the energetic grappling and groping is not so much the green light to go further, but a way of showing your peers that you, too, have what it takes to pull.

For boys, getting off with a girl is vital and the success of the evening is measured entirely by whether they were able to indulge in French kissing in some dark corner. For girls, the essential is to be *seen* doing your kissing – hence the jockeying for prime position on the mattresses laid in strategic positions round the room earlier that day by the Senior Sixth.

In order to acquire the most desirable partner every attention-getting device is used: girls spend three hours perfecting a lavish make-up and fighting over the school hairdryers, boys pose around in dark glasses with hair gelled up, the First Eleven scarf knotted around their necks, asking 'Is there anywhere I can go for a fag – I'm gasping'.

Dances given at girls' schools show much

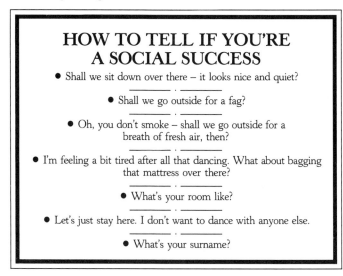

HOW TO TELL IF YOU'RE A SOCIAL SUCCESS

- Shall we sit down over there – it looks nice and quiet?
- Shall we go outside for a fag?
- Oh, you don't smoke – shall we go outside for a breath of fresh air, then?
- I'm feeling a bit tired after all that dancing. What about bagging that mattress over there?
- What's your room like?
- Let's just stay here. I don't want to dance with anyone else.
- What's your surname?

more signs of effort made. The day of the dance is spent decking the School Hall (which doubles as gymnasium) with silver foil to hide the parallel bars, and clustering balloons on the end of looped-up ropes. At the last minute, the Senior Sixth strew rubber gym mats, mattresses, sagbags and all the floor cushions from the House sitting room round the Hall and its environs. The food is better than at boys' schools because it is made by the cookery class but the drink is weaker – watered red wine punch with bits of cucumber floating in it which visiting boys try and lace with bottles brought in their pockets. Although all the trying-on of clothes, make-up, shoes and new faces has been done the previous night amidst much speculation and giggling, getting ready still takes a good three hours.

Everything starts very properly before going over the top. At 7.30 the bus rolls up with its cargo of boys at the peak of their most virile years, now temporarily away from their monastic second home, to be greeted by the primly polite reception line of girls at the school front door. At boys' schools, the boys stand waiting, tapping their feet and looking cool while saying to each other 'I give that one five' before moving in on the good girls, but at girls' schools there are stilted conversations, invariably beginning with some question about A-levels (at that moment, the last thing on anyone's mind) on the short journey to the bar. Insecure girls detailed to act as hostess to a group choose wet-looking boys whom they correctly assume will be terrified of them: everyone is overawed by the goodlooking.

Once at the bar, boys cluster round it like bees, drinking as much and as quickly as they can to pluck up courage. At boys' schools, drink is always stronger to start with and punch made even more lethal by the tipping in of bottles of whisky, gin and vodka surreptitiously bought on trips to the nearest shops: sometimes boys pluck up so much courage they are sick over a girl or two and the following year drink is banned, with the consequence that the party is a disaster.

After the disco has been playing away to the empty floor between the two groups for about an hour, some inaudible signal propels the sexes towards each other and in a few frenzied seconds of competition, cutting in and cutting out, request, rejection and acceptance, pairing is finally achieved and everyone is dancing. An hour later, they are all on the mats or – if it is the boys' territory – disappearing into the carpentry shop or across the rugby pitch.

When the dance finishes around 11.30, there are great cries of 'Where's Charlotte?', until she suddenly appears with ruffled hair from the rhododendron shrubbery and charges onto the coach. At girls' schools, rows of 13-year-olds lean out of upper windows as the Sixth kiss their evening's partners goodnight, exclaiming with high-pitched shrieks 'Oh my *God* – look – that's my Head of House!' Next day, there is no trace of the evening's festivities except for the words 'Sarah Shelley loves Tim Brocklebank' scratched on the Head's dais. But the gossip lasts for weeks.

The letter

Unlike most communications, its news content is irrelevant. Neither side is in the least interested in the other's chances in the French exam; what they want is a status symbol to wave in front of envious peers ('Look what I got today!') or leave lying casually on the table so that the giveaway postmark can be seen. The medium *is* the message, and the recipient's smugness level correlates almost exactly to that of the passion expressed in the precious missive, later to be handed round the class and shown to trusted friends (anyone who can be counted on not to taunt you mercilessly with the contents on a future occasion).

One interesting feature of the school love letter – which frequently arrives by the sackful on the first Tuesday after the School Dance – is that although each one is read by at least a dozen people, neither party ever realises the other is passing theirs around in exactly the same way . Occasionally, this is

---

SARTORIAL SIGNALS

In the teens, clothes are a code used to indicate status, popularity, achievement, outlook on life and where you're at sexually. From the First Fifteen rugger shirt and the fancy waistcoats worn by members of Pop to the right haircut, trainers, bangle or cut of trousers for holiday wearing, clothes make loud and unmistakable statements to friends, enemies and potential lovers. At school, emphasis is on variations from the uniform; in the holidays, with limited means, it's vital to reach the compromise of being part of a group and yet standing out from it – only with the right clothes can you crash the really trendy parties, attract the right love object. No wonder teenagers take so long in the bathroom.

discovered, often through an aforesaid 'trusted' friend who lets slip some telling and identifiable phrase, and a huge row ensues with fierce recriminations ('How DARE you show my letter to your creepy little friends!'), details of which naturally go round the immediate circle and are passed on in due course to the more distant outer rings. By letter.

The teenage bop

Teenage Balls (age range: 13–18) like the Feathers or the Blizzard are an important rite of passage. They mark the social début of the adolescent boy or girl and, though ostensibly a mini version of adult balls – black ties or theme outfits, dinner parties beforehand, your own table once there – are a far more significant event to the adoles-

cents who throng them. For one thing, it is often the newly-teenaged boy or girl's first experience of dancing in public. Everyone wants their school mentioned or record played, every sign of precocious sexual activity is noted by groups of little 13-year-old girls standing round the edge of the dance floor screaming to each other 'Look, look, Rory McTavish just put his hand on Camilla Penrose's bottom!', but what really distinguishes them is the energy level. No one is still for more than five seconds and then only to light a cigarette – high-pitched squeals cut effortlessly through the steadily mounting decibel count and even the older teenagers, who have tanked up beforehand at more grown-up dinner parties only manage briefly to look sophisticated and bored before the general pubertal frenzy gets to them too.

Next day, playgrounds buzz and telephone lines are red hot: those who had a bad time are jubilantly taunted by their more successful friends, who in their turn are put down with jibes at the previous evening's partner ('Yeuch!') – and everyone lives on the memory for weeks.

Status symbols

'Every schoolboy's room has either motorbikes, pop stars or nudes on the walls, and often all three. The more motorbikes and nudes you put up in your room, the more you feel you've actually got a motorbike and a nude.'
Boy, 14.

Incredibly important and in essence a crude and explicit version of later indicators of power and wealth – with one major difference. Not for the adolescent the understatement implied by a discreet glimpse of an expensive watch; what you've got is flaunted all the time, be this a powerful motorbike or the rugger shirt, cricket jersey or school scarf that show you've got a boy friend(s).

Other status symbols are getting into pubs well under age, going to pubs so near the school there is a real risk of prefect or patrolling master picking you up, being rich or being a lord – there are always plenty of peer groupies. Wheels are important: girls gain status by going out with a boy who has a car, boys who pass the driving test at 17

Best presents

From a boy, a gold chain for the birthday is a sure winner, with its mixture of obvious cost and symbolism. Girls give records, clothes or joke presents.

Best approach

If it's that time of year, nothing beats the Valentine card plus a little careful leaking to breach the anonymity. (At boys' schools with sixth form girls, it is

THE BEST

a common sight to see boys sneaking round desks to compare the handwriting in a girl's notebook with the one on their Valentine envelope.)

Best kind of photograph

Forget blown-up portraits – they're *boring*. It's okay (i.e. not soppy) to carry round a passport photograph of the loved one, especially if it's the instant variety that come in sheets of four from those curtained cubicles in undergrounds. Neatest of all is one of these showing the two of you together – one to be carried by each of you.

find it gives an extra mileage ingredient to their pulling power.

But the status symbol supreme to flash around, giving bonus points far above anything else, is an older, richer member of the opposite sex. For boys particularly, the Older Woman (and to a boy of 16, a girl of 18 *is* a woman of the world) is both sex object extraordinary and desirable property. Apart from the relief of no hassles about getting home by midnight or rows with irate parents, the boy who manages not just to go out with a woman of 25–30 but to *maintain the relationship* is considered capable de tout – Mr Supercool himself.

2 Love in Academe

The most instantly noticeable sociological feature of academic love is that it is just about the only kind conducted without benefit of the telephone. Campus call boxes tend to be either crowded, as in the richer universities, with students ringing the parental home for five minutes of tightly-packed communication ('I'll be back next Friday evening with all my laundry, could you ring Jane, Freddie and Camilla, oh and my tape deck's broken . . .') before handing over the handset to the next impatient caller; or vandalised by students expressing their disapproval of some aspect of Government policy.

For the shy boy, then, there is the hideous prospect that girls must be approached face to face: no chance of hiding the tingling face or sweating palms behind the anonymity of the telephone cord. Many take refuge in brief notes, passed with an impassive face over the top of reading desk or table; sometimes, exceptionally gifted notewriters find their talents pressed into service by friends like the letter writer in an Indian village. Rows of little notes on a female mantelpiece are the equivalent of a beltful of dangling scalps.

Others avoid the trauma of the first move by a carefully contrived juxtaposition of seats in the more casual setting of lecture hall or tutorial. Mysterious changes of course halfway through a term often betoken a sad footnote to these attachments: something has gone so badly wrong that the jilted can no longer bear to sit next to the jiltee in the close proximity of private seminar or tutorial.

Getting fresh

The first week of the first term is All Change Week. Girl or boy friends from the freshman's previous existence are chucked, and new allegiances made. Some manage to find a new attachment almost before they go up, groping through the smoke, gloom and noise of the Freshers' Party in the college cellar for the nearest attractive stranger to latch on to. Because it's recognised that freshman need a little time to find their feet, the abortive first-term affair is known merely as a cul-de-sack and no disgrace is attached to such promiscuity. At Oxbridge this is sometimes regularised into orthodoxy via a points system: so much for someone lured in to coffee, so much for hand-holding, and gold star rating to anyone found in bed with a girl by the Scout or Bedder the following morning.

During the first year, university love is frequently subject to the forceful influence of visibility. Most first-year students are crowded together in dormitory blocks; thanks to the delights of modern architec-

T·H·E P·H·A·L·L·I·C P·U·N·T P·O·L·E

As always, the Oxbridge undergraduate is privileged: punting is the perfect first step in this ritual mating dance. Lighthearted, romantic and yet non-commital, it has the delicious bonus for the sexually insecure in that it reinforces instinctive stereotypes – the male upright, active and in control, the female spread out submissive and willing at his feet, with the powerful phallic symbolism of the punt pole only adding to this charming picture. With all these advantages, Oxbridge undergraduates tend to make commitments that last throughout university life. (NB, Second and Third years punt purposefully up the river to moor in their favourite backwater surrounded by a forest of near-impenetrable reeds where the only surprise is caused by another couple with similar intentions.)

ture even the minimal privacy afforded by these rows of identical cells is often eroded – St Hilda's, Oxford, for instance, has an all-glass block which allows passers-by a good look in at the girls' doings (hence the well-known Oxford proverb 'People in glass houses can't afford to take high moral tones').

But it isn't until the end of the first year that things really begin to hum. The mistakes of the first term or two are forgotten, unsuitable alliances abandoned, and the serious business of finding a partner for the rest of university life starts; and with the exams that many faculties take at the end of the second term over, the summer stretches ahead, invitingly free.

As the balmy breath of late spring hits the campus, it is as if some invisible, ubiquitous aphrodisiac has been scattered like pollen into every nook and cranny. Guernseys are shed, sleeves rolled up, flesh bared, shoes removed; college doctors, in general a body of elderly men with walrus moustaches, seize every opportunity to ask female undergraduates to remove their clothing; students themselves lie about in pairs on immemorial lawns or remove the 'Keep Off The Grass' notices from the greenswards of newer establishments.

The academic

Many approach sex in the way they approach clearing the rubbish ('well, *someone's* got to do it and it must be my turn by now'), as a matter of hygiene and habit rather than through any burning urge, although a small and active minority go a long way towards correcting any impression of reluctance.

But the main ethos of academic life is undoubtedly work, by which is meant educating yourself rather than those you are paid to teach. Indeed, the higher and more illustrious the post, the less the contact with its raw material in the shape of the students.

Even the traditional subfusc can be subverted by the determined.

Many academics manage to avoid such annoying interference from one term's end to another, the truly beady combining amorous adventure with self-education – I mean, of course, work – in the form of the various academic conferences being held almost constantly at some point around the globe.

Forehead play

As intellectual work, not sex, is the main motivating force of the academic's life, the critical dimension in the academic physique is the size of the forehead rather than that of the sexual member. In any confrontation, aggressive and competitive academics thrust their foreheads foward in the same way butch 19-year-old males (many of them the academic's students) thrust the crotch of their skintight jeans forward with a threatening pelvic swagger, while academics being photographed or arguing always remove their spectacles to allow a clearer view of this *massif frontale.*

By contrast, as anyone who has made even a brief study of professorial boards will tell you, the trousers worn by academics are

'To Pure Mathematics – and may they never be of use to anyone!'
SENIOR WRANGLER'S TOAST

'To Logical Positivism in Munich, the New Celibacy in Chicago, and Modern Languages in New York – and may I score at all of them!'
SENIOR WANGLER'S TOAST

extraordinarily loose, with generous folds, impromptu pleats, and a crotchpiece worn somewhere between the knees, all of which suggests the sexual negativity of a skirt.

Much of this vague cloaking effect finds its way into academic speech. Used as he is to crawling around the frontiers of knowledge with a hand lens, the academic can seldom say anything straightforwardly, let alone when working up to a difficult request like asking a woman out to dinner.

'I'm so sorry to bother you' is a characteristic beginning. 'I'm quite aware that I may sound very much like one of those people who come up to other people and say to them "I wonder if there's any possibility we could go out tonight?"

'Naturally, the last thing I would want is to be mistaken for someone who might make any such predictable, not to say banal, approach. Especially – and let me put this on record straightaway – as in many ways I find the whole notion of courtship ludicrous when set in the context of the psychological and emotional needs of men and women in present-day society, let alone when viewed in any kind of comparative way. Even if one merely touches on the wealth of

anthropological material at our disposal – though as you know, of course, anthropology is not my subject! – it is clear that different societies have interpreted the possibilities of what we call courtship in such widely differing ways that the very notion of entering such a ritual is shot through with ideas of cultural relativity . . . but I digress. Would you happen to be free for dinner tonight?'

The post-coital seminar

Once past this initial hurdle, another quickly looms. Academics are one of the very few groups in society today likely to be either talking about or making notes on the act they are engaged in. People from the outside world are often surprised to find the academic pausing in the middle of some particularly effective piece of foreplay to jot down a cryptic sentence or two, sometimes to serve later as the basis for a scholarly monograph, occasionally merely out of habit (trendy academics or those in the newer faculties such as Computer Studies mutter into bedside tape recorders). After making love, academics sometimes conduct a post-coital seminar on the orgasm. As the only person sympathetic to this attitude is another academic, this may go some way towards explaining the prevalence of homosexuality at many universities.

If the academic is (uncharacteristically) silent, he is probably Thinking. Academics Think all the time. Unlike coalmining, typing or playing a musical instrument, Thinking is not an activity incompatible with making love, so the academic gazing wistfully across the dinner table is not necessarily expressing interest in the face opposite; he is probably pondering the latest thoughts on structuralism. Many academics have brought Thinking to such a fine art, they can bestow passionate kisses while turning over Chomsky's recent revisions on the Theory of Language in their heads.

That ghastly woman

Another fact that should always be borne in mind is that the academic world is male-dominated. At the time of writing there isn't a single woman Vice Chancellor in the country and only about six per cent of professors are female. Given the inordinate jealousy, suspicion and insecurity endemic in the academic world, it is hardly surprising that any female who does achieve academic distinction is invariably known as 'that ghastly woman'. Nor that, unless jolted by sudden passion, very little sexual activity goes on between the academic man and the academic woman.

Partly this is because even beautiful academic women, in an effort at self-protection due to their heavy outnumbering by male colleagues, tend to shroud themselves in enormously unbecoming clothes; partly it is because of the academic's habit of darting into the womblike security of his study at the first hint of any untoward disturbance in the air. Part lair, part workplace, part security blanket, this room is the only part of the academic house considered essential. Indeed most academics see their houses as studies with attached bedrooms and kitchens, and should the academic wife fail to provide for a study when doing up the house, the academic will remedy this oversight by laboriously carrying armfuls of books and papers into whatever chamber he considers most suitable for long periods of occupancy. Usually this is the lavatory, which explains why all academic houses have proper studies.

Summer cum laude

Hard as it is to imagine eroticism and Milton Keynes in the same breath, the saturnalia of the academic world are undoubtedly the Open University's summer seminars.

Most O.U. students are around 40, full of memories of what it was like to be young in the Sixties and determined to recreate this mood while away from the sobering influence of husband, wife, children or dog. On the afternoon the school starts, car parks are loud with the sound of slamming boots as men pull the baby carriage out of the back seat and hide it in the boot, while indoors a regular clinking signifies that women are taking off their wedding rings preparatory to hiding the telltale white mark with Mantan.

GUILTY OFFENDERS

The first evening is devoted to pairing off: speed is of the essence as most schools only last a fortnight. Habitués are first down to the bar and in the dining room grab the coveted table near the door so they can have first crack at the available talent. In the early mornings, telephone booths are full of men looking furtively round while saying: 'Hullo, Miranda, this is Daddy speaking. Are you being a good girl and eating up your muesli?'. The last afternoon is devoted to a present-buying orgy (as opposed to the other kind which has been going on all week) as guilt swoops in before the return home.

At some schools, usually those covering the more abrasive subjects, a heady whiff of competitiveness streaks the sex-soaked atmosphere. Students with exceptional pulling power go round with smug expressions and little course badges on their clothes to indicate the number of tutors they've been able to bag, rather as pilots used to paint swastikas on the sides of their Spitfires, while those whose main talents lie in extra-curricular activities achieve the coveted rating, *summer cum laude.*

Academics and students

Every academic can see why it's profoundly undesirable to sleep with someone you are going to assess. 'It's not only that I won't be able to give Jennifer a Third if that's all she deserves' runs the reasoning, 'but also that if she deserves a First no one will believe she's got it honestly.'

Thus many affairs between academics and students are initiated by the student. Apart from the younger and rowdier dons, the academic's habitual tendency to view every proposed action from all sides and then remain frozen into immobility by the counter-pulling of the various arguments going on inside his head is aggravated by his knowledge of the awkward position the student will find herself in if he makes an approach and she says No. Students have no such inhibitions, and their only worry is how to make their feelings known without attracting the attention of their fellows.

The favourite place for doing this is anywhere where seating is arranged roughly on classroom lines. Here the student can smoulder, gaze or pout her lips in a kiss with only the lecturer, facing them all, aware of what she is doing. Those who wish to concentrate on some attractive young don will sit in the front row, giving languorous glances, slowly and suggestively crossing their legs or sucking their pencils until the poor man is driven to distraction. Male students taken with a pretty young tutor often ask her out to dinner on the pretext of saying 'Thank You' when what they really mean is 'Please'.

Even the traditional subfusc (the regulation black and white worn for Oxbridge examinations) can be subverted by the determined woman undergraduate: instead of black tie, white skirt, black skirt and stockings, garments such as white boob tubes, black leather minis, black lace tights and studded black leather collars have been seen.

For the susceptible lecturer, such invita-

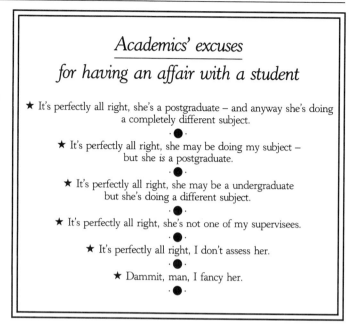

**Academics' excuses
for having an affair with a student**

★ It's perfectly all right, she's a postgraduate – and anyway she's doing a completely different subject.

·●·

★ It's perfectly all right, she may be doing my subject – but she *is* a postgraduate.

·●·

★ It's perfectly all right, she may be a undergraduate but she's doing a different subject.

·●·

★ It's perfectly all right, she's not one of my supervisees.

·●·

★ It's perfectly all right, I don't assess her.

·●·

★ Dammit, man, I fancy her.

·●·

tions are hard to resist. Quite apart from the delicious knowledge of the jealousy he is inspiring in colleagues by his impact on some young and beautiful creature, by sleeping with a student a teacher can learn things no one would dare to tell him otherwise, including what is most interesting of all, the dirt on his own colleagues – which senior member of staff approaches all the most nubile freshmen for photographic sessions, which lecturer identifies the object of his desire and is then so abrasive to everyone else that eventually she is the only one left in his tutorials, who is considered the college dreamboat.

Many of these affairs end in marriage, for what more tempting prospect to the masculine ego than a young, pretty and intelligent woman who looks up to you adoringly? If his bride has managed to gain her degree before the wedding, they may wind up as a formidable academic couple complementing each other's studies or lecturing at the same university; if not, she will probably become . . .

The academic wife

Most academics appear to have picked up their wives absentmindedly, almost unconsciously, during their progress through higher degrees, interdepartmental struggles and the race for publication, rather as someone walking through rough countryside finds that a burr has been attached to his clothing for some time.

Some of these wives were the academic's student married during those halcyon days in the Sixties when students were fair game and the academic divorce rate consequently enormous. Today breakups are few, largely because academics have reverted to their original pattern of scarcely noticing whether they are married or not.

Academic custom encourages this attitude. In Oxbridge, social life is designed for the single male. Even the phrase most commonly used 'he has a wife', instead of the ordinary world's 'he's married', is designed to float the idea of the wife as an academic wife is out in the country: academics feel they can work better in some leafy and undisturbed surrounding. Here, living in some rural converted slum called 'The Old Piggery' or 'The Stables', she bakes her own bread, chauffeurs her husband when he feels the urge to visit his place of employment (few academics drive), gives occasional dinner parties and joins the University Wives' Society. At its meetings she discusses recipes, household hints and playgroup rotas with other similarly-abandoned females, and is reassured to discover that their husbands, too, react exactly the same way ('I'm going into my study') to any sudden or alarming suggestions, be they serious conversation or impromptu sex.

Styles

There is considerable evidence for the theory that both student and professorial styles of lovemaking are affected by the faculty they happen to be in. Economists, for exam-

&&Does once on a Thursday count as twice on a Saturday night? ""

ple, go into a cost benefit analysis while in bed ('I'm fairly tired ... but on the other hand, we haven't done it for some days now'), or alternatively think in terms of credit possibilities 'Does once on a Thursday count as twice on a Saturday night?' They lie in bed calculating far into the night, until the snores of their partner convince them that all such activity is – well, academic.

encumbrance that has to be coped with. So wives who are ideal dinner party material – beautiful, witty, intelligent, outgoing – find themselves left at home night after night as their husband succumbs more or less willingly to the pressure to stay in college for the evening until he finally attains that coveted and approving encomium 'a good college man'.

In other universities, the place of the

Geographers are more interested in contours than conversation; lawyers invariably ask if there's been a precedent. Budding politicians always shake hands first and historians say 'That's one for the archives!'.

The teaching staff are equally affected. Music professors, as with musicians generally, keep up the chase until retiring age and for all anyone knows, well past it. Some get so carried away they urge their partners on with cries of 'allegro ma non troppo' at three in the morning (the only answer here is to bang on the wall with a cry of 'piano!'). One notorious professor of music went so far as to install a waste disposal unit in his kitchen as an alibi: its grunts and roars almost exactly matched his own. 'Just clearing up after a late snack' he would explain innocently to enraged or jealous colleagues in the neighbouring rooms.

Sociologists remember the good times from the Sixties and try to recreate them with thoroughly unsuitable students – the lecturers are the ones crammed into jeans, saying 'Far out!', clicking their fingers to old Pink Floyd records and even in some cases rolling their own cigarettes, while the students, wearing suits and the blandly noncommittal expression of the trained observer, practise for the outside world by keeping an expression of polite interest on their faces whatever the circumstances.

In the newer faculties like accountancy and information technology where the younger lecturers and professors are found (collectively known as *New Blood*) both staff and students are frequently in love with their computers, giving them pet names and sneaking in after dark to play with them or, in some cases, confide in them. Occasionally the more organised male students will key in the names of girls who DO, in a floppy-disk version of the little black book, which the more unscrupulous lecturers later run off on their daisy wheel printers.

Apart from small, randy Welsh professors of whatever discipline who are famous for their pursuit of women (surprisingly, these are never the ones that charges of sexual harassment are brought against), undoubtedly those most influenced by sex in its broadest and most generalised form are the English faculties. Most of English Literature is, after all, about love or lust in one form or another.

Some, exposed to too much D. H. Lawrence at an early age, think of themselves as

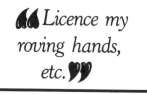

Licence my roving hands, etc.

People of the Loins, believing that some dark force beyond their control is propelling them irresistibly towards the nearest comely member of the opposite sex; others, suffused with the romantic poets, see the tremulous beginnings of flirtation even in the metronome voice of the speaking clock. The only difference between lecturers and students is that the former tend to stick to well-chosen if obscure texts before grabbing while students prefer Donne's invaluable 'Licence my roving hands, etc.'

May Balls

This Oxbridge phenomenon is at once institution, party, glamour festival and financial drain of the year, the stuff of which memories are made and sexual litmus test.

What staggers everyone is where the money comes from. Undergraduates who have survived on the minimum grant fork out £100-plus for a double ticket; girls disappear to London to return with £500 ball dresses which by 7.30 the following morning have picked up grass stains from the college lawn or trailed through the waters of the Cam or Cherwell in the traditional punt up river for breakfast.

Attractive girl undergraduates juggle with invitations debating whether it is safe to refuse A in case B doesn't come up to scratch. Plain ones pray they'll be asked or hope friends will fix them up with a blind date.

May Balls also bring out the female undergraduate's particular *bête noire:* the girls from the secretarial colleges that surround university towns. These are usually prettier, often richer, spend endless time on clothes and make-up and, untroubled by feminist notions of equality, have no scruples at using every feminine wile available to attract and flatter the susceptible male undergraduate. The female undergraduate's self-respect will not allow her to take on these pests at their own game – yet how to convince a callow 19-year-old boy that good conversation is preferable to the most lusciously lip-glossed of inanities? No wonder that for many these festivities are known as Maybe Balls.

WHERE (Oh, where?)

Bulking large in any academic affair is the problem of The Bed. Although those in the academic world are in the exquisite position of being able to make love at any time of day they want – it is very seldom that either student or lecturer actually *has* to be at a given place at a given moment – choice of venue is often a complication.

The trouble is that student beds are narrower than any other known to man. Many are believed to have been early models for the idea of the Japanese capsule hotel, only

The band seems to have stopped while we were talking – and it's only 6.30.

> ❦❦ Student beds are narrower than any other known to man ❦❦

reluctantly discarded by the Japanese themselves on the grounds of their extraordinary discomfort. Older colleges add even further deterrents: the rooms themselves are cold, draughty, miles from the nearest bathroom and if possible overlooked, while many of the beds themselves are fitted, so the enraged owners believe, with special creaking mechanisms activated instantly by the mere proximity of a body of the opposite sex.

The problem remains even when the student happens to be having an affair with a lecturer rather than a fellow student. For taking a student to an hotel is unthinkable, as the essence of such affairs is that both must believe that they have suddenly been overcome by ungovernable passion. Besides, no academic can afford hotels.

There is, of course, the academic's room. Though few academics are troubled by the luxury of a secretary, so there is little chance of Miss Primley breezing in and out, this is still unsatisfactory. Not because of the danger of possible interruption – all academics respect each other's obsessive need for secrecy – but because, thanks to the clutter of books and papers which must NOT be moved, horizontal space is frequently limited. Also, by some mysterious process of thought transference, however deserted the corridors appear to be everyone knows

exactly how long both of you have been in there together.

What's left is the student's bed in the student's living quarters. As only the far-sighted or the determinedly promiscuous get themselves fixed up with wider beds (requesting one on the medical grounds of back injury is considered the safest ploy), the unhappy lecturer soon discovers that going to sleep after the act is only possible either on top of or alternatively underneath the student. So little does this fit in with the academic's mental processes that many lecturers consider getting out of bed and lying on the floor beside the student, ignominious as it is, to be preferable. An hour in this chilly and uncomfortable posture is considered sufficient to indicate caringness.

The library

The importance of the library in campus romance can never be overestimated. In these dark and intimate places, the rule of silence causes whispered conversations between couples who are forced to stand close together to hear what each is saying. Notes inviting assignations are dropped into laps; by dint of watching like hawks, shy male students can slide into the seat next to the beautiful stranger the moment it becomes vacant. Comment Books, meant for suggestions like 'Why is there only one copy of Monypenny and Buckle's *Disraeli?*' are filled instead with remarks like 'Who is the gorgeous blonde in Seat 24?'

There are plenty of opportunities for being alone; and the obscurer the subject, the less likely anyone is to disturb you behind the ceiling-high shelves. Many library shelves are stacked in alleys, each separately lit, and here the prosaic light cord is an object of the most delicate erotic nuance: 'forgetting' to pull it to On is an implicit sign of willingness, while giving it a hasty jerk as you round the corner is a firm 'Hands off.'

In some libraries, students take the word 'Silence' so literally that the obverse – 'Anything goes as long as you don't make a noise' – has come to be equally accepted, with everything from handholding to advanced petting going on as a matter of course. One at Oxford is well known as a rendezvous for long kissing sessions between those who have no intention of taking a book out; and occasionally, late at night, the more daring put the floor to use. (Law libraries, for some esoteric reason, are considered to have a particularly favourable atmosphere for all sorts of sexual manifestations.)

For the lecturer with seduction in mind, a tour of the library ('Let me show you where the Early Sanskrit texts are kept') is an ideal way of testing the water. Where an invitation to enter the lecturer's study could make a student feel awkward, threatened or resentful, the library is neutral ground – nevertheless, its aphrodisiac powers are so well known that Librarianspeak for an attractive man is 'I wouldn't mind getting him behind the 920s'.

A Magdalene don of divinity
Had a daughter who kept her virginity.
The fellows of Magdalene
Must have been dagdalene
It wouldn't have happened at Trinity . . .

Third year students take the Library seriously.

3 The Post-Deb Set

Post-deb people live in Chelsea, Fulham, Battersea, Wandsworth and, especially for P-D's who marry each other, Clapham; but the real pounding heart of the Post-deb set is Parson's Green (Ceroc ball organiser James Cronin says that of the 5,000 addresses on his list almost 90 per cent have an SW6 postcode). Here, inside every delicatessen, girls called Fiona or Minty buy cartons of taramasalata, streets are littered with Golfs, Sciroccos and Renault fives – all the area the Tube doesn't

make boxer shorts or crackers with *decent* presents inside is a typical P-D good idea.

P-D boys talk about drink all the time – 'we're talking beer now'(i.e., going to the pub), 'I was seriously drunk last night' – while girls warn each other about P-D boys who are 'dangerous' (i.e. untrustworthy with women but glamorous with it). All the girls are on the Pill but there are still hundreds of abortions, and though everyone talks about herpes, AIDS is never mentioned. Having an overdraft is cool and so is being exhausted – shows what a good time you're having – though merely feeling tired is Boring.

Coming to maturity in Fulham

Many Post-debs – especially those fresh from expensive boarding schools – only graduate to Fulham after an early start in some squalid semi-commune north of the Park, in places like Ladbroke Grove or Frithville Gardens, where groups of up to ten share large rooms or whole floors of an old house. Here the washing-up is never done, impromptu drink parties for 300 are a weekly happening, the front door is regularly broken by some occupant or friend with drink on board and keys forgotten, and £500 phone bills go unpaid. Tripping over couples entwined on the floor is a minor hazard, and nobody bats an eyelid if there are three extra to breakfast. Eventually, when the filth, constant borrowing, problems with hot water and thought of the inevitable nemesis (being thrown out yet again after one all-night party too many) outweigh the fun, the fizzy conversations, the feeling of being into life at last, the incipient Post-deb person moves out of this chrysalis stage and into full Fulham maturity.

Often the trigger is simply sleeplessness.

Some day my prince will come ... kindergarten teaching is a favourite occupation in PD-land.

go to is reached by GTW instead – greengrocers now stock lychees, celeriac and kiwi fruit, newsagents the FT, Harpers and Country Life. Dustbins clink rather than rustle, and the giant Sainsburys at Vauxhall is a social rendezvous with dinner invitations exchanged at the fresh orange juice counter; and there is an off-licence on every corner. Telephones are red-hot from 6.30 onwards as everyone tries to find out what everyone else is doing or leave a message for James or Camilla to ring back; an answerphone is the sign of a P-D who works from home – starting up a company to

'If there are a lot of you, regularly every night somebody is going to come back drunk at 3.00 a.m., slam the doors and put the music system full on' comments one veteran, 'and by this time you've probably started a job where you *have* to be on time in the morning'.

Once in Fulham (the arty, the media-oriented and those in advertising tend to hive off to more 'colourful' areas like Brixton or Notting Hill Gate), the Post-deb person's life becomes generally more stable though no less frenetic. By now, a network of friends has been formed and, with luck, an 'interesting' job landed, though P-D people never allow the latter to interfere with the real purpose of life: having a good time (on some P-D ski parties, there is a penalty, usually buying drinks all round, for anyone who mentions their job).

As P-D people get older, boys pay more often for girls instead of going Dutch, dinner parties become more important to everyone and more formal, girls start to ask if there is a washing machine in the flat they propose to share, and boys sometimes ask a

---

GOING OUT WITH

- I'm going out with James tonight = I'm going out with James tonight

---

- I'm going out with James = I'm sleeping with James, and we don't mind our friends knowing this.

---

girl direct for her phone number instead of acquiring it by the time-honoured circuitous route of someone who knows a friend of one of her best friends.

Often sexual relationships improve as well. Being pretty, insecure and possibly rich as well, as many Post-deb girls are when they emerge new-minted from boarding school or secretarial college, is a recipe for being walked over, while the more aggres-sive and Army and City men, who know they are eventually going to settle down into marriage and the conventional life, want to have as many girls as possible before that happy day, as quickly as they can. At this stage of her career, what the Post-deb girl has to learn to spot is not so much Mr Right as Mr Rightaway.

♠*Nobody turns a hair provided they don't get Boring* ♥♥

Let's share!

Post-deb people share flats or, increasingly these days, houses (often owned by one of their number). The words 'my flatmate' have a completely non-sexual connotation, and nine times out of ten the relationship is in fact platonic. This is not as difficult as it sounds: since most Post-deb people use their flat only for washing, dressing and the few hours of sleep necessary to sustain life, many go for days at a time without actually seeing a flatmate. In-house standards of modesty maintain the implicit just-good-friends convention, only being occasionally bent by time priorities ('If he's been hogging the bath for hours I'll finally walk in and clean my teeth', 'If she's got her headphones on I'll go into her bedroom and shout "Telephone!"')

In cases where couples do sleep as well as live together, nobody turns a hair provided they don't get Boring (q.v.): that is, giving soppy looks, going on holiday alone together and generally behaving like newly-weds. But for two flatmates to contemplate sharing nights as well as days they have to

'BORING . . .'

A useful adjective to describe anything that acts as a dampener on the idea of group fun; specifically sexual conduct of an exclusive nature.

Public displays of affection such as holding hands, sitting in the cinema with arms around each other, or walking arm-in-arm, are *boring*. Being star-struck lovers is not only *boring* but wet, while sitting on someone's knee is only permissible if you treat it as a chair rather than a chance to gaze into their eyes. It is all right for a couple to show the rapport between them by means of *non-boring* gestures (i.e. those which could pass between any two members of the opposite sex on friendly terms) such as hugs, the odd kiss, plenty of teasing. Since being lovey-dovey is *dead-boring*, Post-debs who want to do the double act for a bit simply drop temporarily out of the group ('he's having a quiet time with her'). Those who want to stay on the social circuit take care not to come across as a twosome, which means going out to dinner separately, dancing with other people at balls and, even if it bores them silly, avoiding any kind of behaviour which could possibly be called *Boring*.

be extra-sure: if the whole thing goes sour after a couple of months, one of you has to go. For the departing one, this can mean not only a busted romance but a traumatic social upheaval as well: most houses – especially those where several great friends live together – are the nucleus of a sizable group of intimates. Breaking off with a loved one is bad enough, but losing a home and group of friends into the bargain! There's only one word to describe it . . . Nightmare!

Problems

The Post-deb version of the Agony Aunt is a close friend of the opposite sex; it is with these confidant(e)s that love problems are chiefly discussed though, because everyone takes such an interest in everyone else's affairs, what's going on is known generally.

NICE GIRLS DO

– BUT *SERIOUSLY*

A girl can have had 10 lovers by the time she's 24 and still be 'nice'. The criterion is that if you sleep with someone it's with the idea of serious commitment – you may find you've made a mistake and withdraw from the relationship, but you *went into it* seriously.

The cardinal sin is cheating (sleeping with someone else when you've already got a girl/boy friend); and the act is hardly complete before the rest of the group know about it – with Post-debs, gossip is the favourite form of afterplay.

Eating

For Post-deb people eating means eating out – on the rare occasions when one of them is in, dinner is a piece of toast – at one of a clutch of favourite restaurants. These are distinguished by their similarities rather than their differences, chief of which is that at any one of them there is the likelihood of bumping into friends. All Post-debs like going to restaurants known to be popular among their friends so that even if none are actually there, there is still the comforting feeling they might be. This impression is fostered by the fact that the boys behind the counter in the wine bar and the waitresses darting between the tables have exactly the same preppy look as the customers (on their days off, many of them *are* the customers). So that down in Fulham you see one type of person only – boys still in their suits or changed into the colourful jersey but always with the striped shirt, girls in jeans or skirts with pearls over their frilled collars and guernseys. Post-debs who occasionally go on safari to Covent Garden or Soho feel as though they are in a foreign country, so heterogeneous are all the faces round them. Fortunately, the natives are usually friendly.

IN PLACES FOR P-D's

Some favourite resturants are:

Pigeons
Foxtrot Oscar
Clowns
Brinkleys
Jakes
Totties
Glaisters
Bon Acceuil

Some favourite clubs are:

Raffles
151
Tramp (except on a Saturday night) and it's terribly chic to go to Annabels constantly, especially if you're not a member.

Drinking

Certain pubs virtually belong to Post-deb people, who treat them as a combination of club, listening post and singles bar. Girls who have just arrived in London for the secretarial course at Queens College go in twos and threes (but never on their own) to the Cod, where they inevitably wind up in a group, locating other girls they've been at school with, or their brothers, with the unerring accuracy of one ball of mercury finding another. Boys drink beer though girls usually stick to wine (girls who don't like to confess to being teetotal sip Ribena), nobody ever admits to feeling hungry, and the evening winds up with invitations to 'come round for a drink'. Next day there is a group at one or other of the flats concerned, drinking cheap plonk as no one can afford spirits. Two or three years on it's easier to predict who frequents which pub on any

given evening, and romantic plans are accordingly laid for 'surprise' meetings with the fancied one.

Pubs are subject to the vagaries of fashion but perennial names are: The Admiral Codrington (The Cod), The Duke of Wellington, The Australian, The Scarsdale, The Antelope (very City-oriented), The Shuckburgh (estate agents, very young girls, loud), The Ship, The Surprise and, still hanging on by a thread, The White Horse.

The Army

Although almost everyone in the Post-deb Set has a link with the Army – brother, cousin, friend or boy friend – Army men are in a league of their own, different from everybody else.

At home, Sandhurst boys can be picked out in any of the bars along the King's Road: they aim to be totally identifiable so put on their brogues and trilbies and make remarks like, 'I was run over by a tank last week' in loud voices. They all have nicknames – Wiggy, Piggy, Tiggy, Puffy, Wuffy, Duffy, Packy, Tacky, Wacky, Dusty, Rusty, or Lusty – and sisters who are cooks or chalet girls. Most spend a lot of time in Germany where they lead a semi-colonial life, seldom

OF COURSE, PIGGY WAS TOTALLY BLOTTO WHEN HE DROVE THE CHIEFTAIN THROUGH THAT SCHOOL BUS

fraternising with the natives and often spending months without seeing a nubile English girl. The result is that women are treated with a heady mixture of old-fashioned chivalry, romantic admiration and simple lust or, on certain other occasions, as playthings – 20 Army men home on leave would hire a couple of call girls for an evening's fooling around where no estate-agent-Nigel would think of it.

The Mess party

Nobody can give a party like the Army. It's the highlight of the year in the Mess and a tremendous amount of energy and organisation goes into it. Other boys get

> **❝ Good fun birds will climb to the top of the marquee in their best ball dress and join in shaving cream fights with shrieks and hoots. ❞**

very jealous – why do the girls have to go out to Germany to find fun, isn't London good enough? – and partly because of the irresistible glamour of the whole thing, which turns every woman into a Scarlett O'Hara kneedeep in men on her verandah, her lightest whim instantly to be gratified. Army boys spring immediately to their feet in chorus every time a women comes into the room, no guest is allowed to put her hand into her own pocket for so much as a packet of duty-free cigarettes and, as the Army boys all know each other so well they play off each other, performing in an often

very witty way as they compete for the attention of their female guests.

As the main deterrent to going to a dance in Germany is the cost of the ticket there, the Army have thoughtfully got round this too. Most of the regiments organise a coach, variously known as the Birdie Bus or the Fluff Wagon, which sets off from outside Peter Jones (where else?) on most Friday afternoons crammed to the brim with Sloanes and a sprinkling of boys – people from other regiments, Army brothers or best friends. Girls stay with the Pads (married couples) writing thank-you letters afterwards to the President of the Mess Committee, who puts them in a file where all the Army boys can leaf through them, as well as privately to whoever has asked them. Another difference between the Army and everyone else is that after the weekend and the dance are over, Army boys discuss the girls far more than the girls discuss them.

The good fun bird

'She's a good fun bird,' is the highest praise Army boys can bestow on a woman. Though where women are concerned, Army men are basically quite easily pleased: the only thing that doesn't go down well is a plain woman and, while Army boys who went to university aren't frightened of career girls – they lived with embryo ones for three years before going to Sandhurst – the others are. 'Oh, I'm so daunted by all you career women,' says the Army boy. Army boys like their girl friends to be uncomplicated, pretty, unfeminist and not particularly bright (thickness runs in many Army families) and good in company, although stunningly beautiful ones can get away with being silent objects of admiration. Above all, though, they must be Good Fun Birds.

Good Fun Birds can take stick, aren't prudes, laugh at the Army boys' jokes, are always on for something 'outrageous' (i.e., noisy) and enjoy being teased about being stupid. Good Fun Birds will climb to the top of the marquee in their best ball dress and join in shaving cream fights with shrieks and hoots. Good Fun Birds never sit around telling Army Boys about Herbalife because that's weirdie, nor do they get depressed – that's neurotic. Nor do they ever, ever get tired because that's *boring*. And if you're even the teeniest, tiniest bit boring – well, you just aren't a Good Fun Bird.

Parties

Parties are the big sexual hunting ground, the major meeting point, the spot to make the kill or the whirlwind strike when everyone else is drunk. In the earlier years, drinks parties are born from a desperation to meet people and set up the friendship circle; once this ring of confidants is established, drinks parties are to keep it in place. So the first priority of all Post-deb people after they have found a flat is to give a drinks party.

If you're a Good Fun Bird, even shaking hands can be hilarious.

Until married respectability sets in these are always of the bring-a-bottle kind; either bring-a-bottle smart (you're asked a week in advance, you dress up a bit, and hope to go dancing as the long day wears into night), or bring-a-bottle relaxed (invitations that morning, come as you are, everything starting and finishing a bit earlier). Girls out hunting never take their bicycles to parties in case they're offered a lift home, boys keep their options open until they reckon they've met a player. At the smart parties there's a lot of coke – champagne, whiskey and coke is the great party mix – but though everyone knows a heroin addict, they're not on the scene: addicts simply aren't interested in courting, and the whole of Post-deb life is about sex in one way or another.

Parties in the country are taken terribly seriously, with people getting very excited about the idea of whizzing down on Friday night and being billeted on a house party, and the non-country-born worrying about the etiquette of it all and what to take.

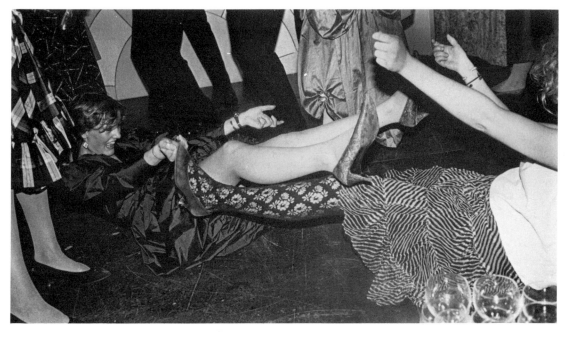

Once there, country parties turn out to be the wildest of all (in London, size is but one of the limiting factors), with gardens, marquees, lavish expenditure and the nooks and crannies of a large house adding to the air of carnival. A party isn't a party without champagne flowing freely all night – those who try and pass off sparkling wine are marked down – and at parties where they're stingy with the champagne, going behind the discotheque will unearth a huge supply of alcohol. Going upstairs is also found at younger P-D parties ('Nanny can't get into her room because there's a couple in the bed'); and just occasionally a maddened father causes a frisson of good behaviour that lasts for several weeks by pulling the plug on the entire party when he finds every counterpane heaving.

The Deejay's tale

'An incredible snobbery surrounds the whole discotheque scene and the higher upmarket you go the more bitchy it becomes, with endless competition about who's doing what party, cashed in on by hosts who know you ('I'd like to book you but I've heard Chatters will give me a better price'). If the favourite discotheque of a really big customer like Sandhurst (all those commissioning balls) blows it, thus leaving the market wide open, there is jubilation all round. A lot of the work comes from who you know, and an incredible snobbery surrounds the whole thing, so you have to flash your connections a bit. If you've got a personality, or someone who's titled, on the disco, or a particularly good girl friend, this may turn you into the flavour of the month – Raffles had John Benson and when Lady Helen Windsor was his girl friend, they were the 'in' disco.

It's very trendy to have your girl friend standing by the disco and girls enjoy the kudos so they usually come. If you *really* want to impress a girl, the thing is to take

OPENING GAMBITS FROM A DEEJAY

★ Like to have a listen through the headphones?

★ Anything you want played?

★ Could you queue up those records for me?

★ Come and help me choose the next one.

★ If that's the one you want, I'm afraid it's back in the van. We'll have to go and hunt for it.

her out in the disco. You're the centre of the whole night, very often you've planned the party and are treated as a guest and invited to the dinner beforehand, you're the complete focus once the evening's started. Disc jockeys are like frustrated pop stars – a lot of them play music themselves so it's the next best thing; and there's the aphrodisiac of being in a position of great power – you can wreck the party merely by playing the wrong music.'

Oh balls!

There are several different types of balls but the best known (to the outside world) are the major annual fixtures like the Caledo-

> **❨❨ *The aphrodisiac of being in a position of great power* ❩❩**

nian, Queen Charlotte's or the Rose Ball; and the big charity hops got up by a Committee, with a Junior Committee of Post-debs who it is hoped will ask all their friends. Then there are the regular, organised balls like the monthly Ceroc dances; as Ceroc hosts are great introducers, dancing with guests who they teach at the

same time, young P-Ds come to these balls as an energetic way of playing the mating game.

About five years ago, a whole new dimension entered the ball scene, when some bright Sloanie realised that even 'proper' balls didn't have to be for charity – *they could just be for other Sloanies!* Now there are hundreds of these, filled by Post-debs in regulation black tie or frilled taffeta according to sex, where absolutely nothing is provided except music and a reasonably stylish place to dance for the £10 or £15 ticket, but everyone goes because everyone goes. Unlike the 'proper' balls, which are phenomenally expensive and where you may only know those in your party, these alternative balls are filled with different groups who link up like overlapping circles. The younger the P-Ds concerned, the cheaper and more over-the-top the ball; for

those at locations like Camden or Hammersmith Palace or warehouses, you come as scruffy as possible – black tie but filthy and all over the place – turning up at 10 p.m. and getting smashed as quickly as possible. After 18 or 19, the idea that the more decadent you can be the more successful the evening begins to pall a bit, and the Post-deb ball enters its most serious phase, becoming what it was originally intended to be: a mating dance.

> ❛❛ *The more decadent you can be, the more successful the evening* ❜❜

4 Love in the Snow

What gives love on the ski slopes its special characteristics is the altitude. A couple of miles higher off the earth's surface, eggs take twice as long to come to the boil but people only half the time. Chalet girls blame all their flops on the altitude ('Can't get a cake to rise at 10,000ft' they say cheerfully); ski bums often make a similar comment though usually in different circumstances. You also get drunk twice as fast high up – the real drinkers are the ones who go home sheet white after a sunny fortnight – but there's only half the hangover. Altitude, it can readily be seen, causes a shift in social behaviour which means anything can happen . . . and it frequently does.

In drag

Speed and competition are the essence of the ski affair. Anyone who is interested in anyone else has to move fast because you are only there for a fortnight, and just about all courting has to be done in the group – in the chalet, the ski class, the restaurant, the bar, the disco. So instead of long wooing talks, ten minutes together on the drag lift is used to extract basic information – are you in love? married? involved? or shall we have lunch? – and cutting a likely prospect out of the herd the most desired social skill.

Ski snobbery

Another aspect of the ski affair is the shake-up it gives to social orientation. Because skiing is what you are all there for, anyone who skis well is high up in the social hierarchy, and therefore a catch. Thus smart Sloanes take up with Australian ski bums, bright girl graduates succumb to the charms of someone whose idea of a good read is the timetable by the skilift (having an affair with the lift man, however, is very

infra dig), and everyone idolises the ski instructor.

As food rather than, for once, drink is pivotal to the ski affair – all that exercise and open air – the chalet girl, bounteous provider and pretty with it, is queen of everyone's dreams. But while chalet girls know that all-male parties will have had bets with each other on the aeroplane as to who can get the chalet girl into bed first, what the punters forget is that chalet girls are now so fit they can ski their way out of trouble any time.

Although everyone is dressed in the same clothes, thus encouraging approachability, there are certain giveaway signs that you are in the presence of a ski aristocrat. Girls who are good skiers can be spotted by the size of their hips – ski muscles tend to produce jodhpur thighs – ski bums by their brown faces with white gogglemarks above a lilywhite frame, and ski instructors, as an

> ❦❦ *Having an affair*
> *with the lift*
> *man is very*
> *infra dig* ❦❦

ever-growing band of the privileged can vouch, by their all-over tans.

It only remains to add that many ski romances only come to full flower after the holiday is over though there is, in the words of one experienced punter, 'an incredible amount of setting-up'. For despite the near-perfect conditions of tingling air, sunshine, marvellous days on the mountain followed by midnight sleigh rides under blazing stars, even the young, single and fighting fit become a trifle daunted by the constant presence of the rest of the group. Or, again, it could be the altitude.

Lothario of the slopes

Ski instructors are very conscious of their image as the resort's walking Adonises and are always burnishing and polishing it. They buy their skipants one size too small so that everything shows up, go to the

---

Opening gambits

- Let me check your bindings.

———— · ————

- We ought to talk about your ski technique but I'll have to make it after class or it won't be fair to the others.

———— · ————

- You're not getting the knees quite right – let me position your legs.

———— · ————

Multigym to develop startling thigh and pectoral muscles, and lie on the hotel sunbed to maintain their tan level when the sun isn't shining. When male punters show up beside them as feeble, unfit and whiteskinned, no ski instructor has ever been known to weep.

Ski instructors know in their bones that all girls coming from abroad are looking for an instant romance. What gives them their air of irresistible, maddening, sexual self-confidence is that girl punters only have a fortnight to achieve this laudable aim ('in Scotland it's often only a long weekend' says one instructor nostalgically) while the ski instructor knows that another crop of Amandas, Carolines and Fionas will turn up like clockwork every week for the next four months. So ski instructors don't have to bother much. Also, playing hard to get makes the girl show her hand – after all, she *has* only got a fortnight.

So when a girl deliberately falls down in front of him, the ski instructor plays it cool and doesn't help her up. 'Stand and watch her struggle for about five minutes until she says "Will you help me?", then go over nonchalantly. Because she thinks you're not interested she's going to try a little harder.'

When a girl asks the ski instructor 'What's the best place to go to at night?' he knows she's really saying 'Will you take me there?' But nothing so crude as the invitation direct escapes the ski instructor's lips; instead, he tells her the name of his favourite bar and adds 'I'm normally there on Wednesdays'. And when the girl and her friend thread their way through the crowd on Wednesday evening and – surprise, surprise! – bump into the ski instructor, he knows he's home and dry.

On the other hand, when it comes to the moment for the first physical move, the ski instructor's reflexes, tuned by all those hours on the mountain, are like Alpine lightning. When a girl the ski instructor fancies falls down accidentally, his superior turn of speed enables him to reach her side before anyone else has so much as flexed

JE T'EMBRASSE, MADELEINE

What the serious ski groupie gives a ski instructor

Rich and glamorous Italian women who zoom up for long weekends while their industrialist husbands are toiling away in the Milan sportswear factory give their longterm ski instructor lovers substantial presents like cars or even flats (though here there is the danger the ski instructor will bring other girls back mid-week). Ski instructors spend most of their time in ski suits so any personal present has to team with this. Most are so health conscious that cigarette cases are out; smart watches and silk neck scarves will do at a pinch but best of all is the hip flask. *ALWAYS* engrave it: 'Je t'embrasse, Madeleine' is a tender reminder and a warning to other women.

their knees; and no one can judge quicker than a ski instructor the precise moment to stop asking about bruises or swellings and start feeling them instead.

To hurry things on, ski instructors may sometimes suggest an evening's tobogganing ('you've got to hang on to me tight'); canny instructors always make sure the toboggan turns over at the end of the run so both of you are flung together in a tangle of arms and legs. And of course, girls who find the drag lift tricky need a steadying arm around their shoulders.

Jeux sans frontières

Ski instructors are even more magnetically attractive across the nationality barrier, especially where English and French are concerned.

'Oh Jean-Pierre, you're so dark and exotic' sighs Camilla from South Ken. 'O Andee, you're so blond and exotique' breathes Marie-France from the Seizième. German girls are not so sought after, and many ski instructors class them as boring; i.e., they come with their families and their fathers will not let them out of sight, let alone into the orbit of a ski instructor. But then, many German girls' fathers were ski instructors themselves.

Just occasionally, a relationship continues

after the fortnight is over – the later on in the season, the more likely this is to happen – and the ski instructor turns up on some expectant Fulham doorstep. But all too often, alas, it is just another case of Hans across the sea.

THE SKI INSTRUCTOR'S DAY

8.00 am The Ski Instructor rises. Checking every instructor's three basics – Teeth, Torso, Tan – in the mirror while he shaves, he notes that the last of these needs some attention. As it is late in the season, he decides on half an hour's sunbathing in the lunch hour, up the mountain (at 10,000 feet, tans come deeper than on any Mediterranean *plage*). Sometimes, reflects the Ski Instructor a trifle wistfully, he wishes he had the natural exhibitionism of his friend Jean-Pierre, who saunters to the middle of the terrace and, waiting until all eyes are on him, unzips his skisuit to reveal a perfectly-muscled body clad only in those minute swimming briefs the French seem to go in for. This performance invariably brings the male punters out in goose pimples of envy and fury and has all the Carolines swooning. As he shoehorns himself into his skintight scarlet skisuit, half a dozen scraps of paper, each one carefully printed in block capitals

For those who want to talent-spot unobtrusively, mirrored sunglasses and a loving pose make the perfect camouflage.

with a name and address, fall like confetti to the floor: the Ski Instructor remembers it was Goodbye Day yesterday.

9.00 am A fresh batch of punters is waiting near the ski lift. So is Jean-Pierre, who is making the most of his few minutes' advantage. Swiftly, the Ski Instructor checks out the talent from behind the mirrored sunglasses that conceal his eyes (often, these are swivelled at right angles to the direction he appears to be looking). After the usual preliminaries, the punters are set to skiing down the nearest slope, ostensibly to allow assessment of their varying capabilities but in reality to let the two instructors take turns at picking the prettiest girls for their respective classes, a custom which reminds the Ski Instructor of picking football teams at school, and Jean-Pierre of choosing a harem.

10.00 am The class are being taught ski lift technique, and the Ski Instructor is employing one of his own well-tried ploys. 'Come on, Caroline' he says to the best-looking blonde in the class. 'We'll give them a lead. The rest of you – pair up and follow on behind us. I'll be waiting for you at the top.'

How fortunate, reflects the Ski Instructor for the umpteenth time, as Caroline comes out with the phrase that is music to all ski instructors' ears 'I'm here with a girl friend' that ski lifts impose an arbitrary time limit. Its ten-minute run means that girls in search of a little light romance know they have no time to waste in getting all the facts clear – he has lost count of the number of times girls have asked him if he is married (he has a girl friend in England but does not feel it is either necessary or relevant to mention this) and confided that No, they themselves have just broken it off with their boy friend. 'What a pity,' thinks the Ski Instructor, glancing at Caroline, that his Golden Rule

EXCUSES … EXCUSES

The Ski Instructor's
never-fail excuse

- I'm sorry, I work
  behind the bar in
  the evenings.

- I'm sorry, I've got
  some races tomorrow
  and I need an
  early night.

Ski buffs.

Number One is: Never have an affair with someone in your own class.

12.00 am Break for lunch. The class flock round the Ski Instructor clamouring to buy him a drink, buy him lunch. Though not a conceited man, the Ski Instructor realises the process of idolisation has begun: it is a well known law of nature that poor skiers worship good ones. Caroline manages to sit next to him; Jean-Pierre, he notices, has homed in on a nearby blonde German girl. Alas, an enormous German boy appears within a couple of minutes and Jean-Pierre, muttering something about bindings, withdraws. This is one of the troubles with the French, thinks the Ski Instructor a trifle complacently; they seldom bother to do that

essential background preparation but jump right in with both feet – ten minutes alone with Gretchen on the ski lift and *he* would have known she was out here with a boy friend – result: five minutes into his chat-up and up comes Franz, 7ft 5in and broad with it, and poor old Jean-Pierre has to move over.

4.00 pm The class are flagging as their unaccustomed muscles take the strain. 'Who's for some glühwein?' suggests the Ski Instructor, who has agreed with Jean-Pierre they will all meet at a pitstop. Because of Golden Rule Number One, he plans to deflect Caroline towards Jean-Pierre, who has a penchant for tall blondes. 'My friend – that's him, the dark handsome one over there – really really likes you but he's too shy to talk to you' he says, using the time-honoured formula, while imperceptibly catching Jean-Pierre's eye. 'Oh, hallo, Jean-Pierre, this is Caroline from England,' he adds with a note of surprise as Jean-Pierre walks past on his way to the bar. As he sips his glühwein and listens to Jean-Pierre getting to work with the old Cointreau accent, the consciousness of having performed a friendly action for two nice people warms the Ski Instructor's heart.

5.30 pm The Ski Instructor is having a quiet drink in one of his favourite bars. As he gazes absentmindedly at the various merry groups around him, a goodlooking woman who has been eyeing him from her vantage point of a bar stool, catches sight of the white instructor's flash on his skisuit. She slides off the stool, approaches him and asks if he gives private instruction. 'I'll pay for it,' she adds, looking at him boldly. Not for the first time, the Ski Instructor reflects that married women are in many ways more appealing than an endless diet of Fionas: somehow they manage to combine

For the Ski Instructor, good things often come in twos.

prietorial – and after all, she does pay the rent of Jean-Pierre's handsome flat. 'What's happened?' asks a plaintive voice; Caroline, bewildered, is tugging at his sleeve. 'Someone broke a leg on the mountain' says the Ski Instructor automatically, employing the classic all-purpose excuse all ski instructors learn at their mother's knee. 'At *this* hour?' says Caroline incredulously. 'We've only just heard' says the Ski Instructor hastily; Caroline, he realises, must quickly be distracted if she is not to a) ask more awkward questions or b) find Jean-Pierre even more irresistible at this evidence of his bravery. The Ski Instructor sets to work.

challenge with a perfectly clear declaration of intent. The Ski Instructor buys this one a drink and settles down to the opening moves of an enjoyable conversation which will end, as she manages subtly to inform him in the first few moments, when her husband returns in half an hour or so from his day in the high mountains.

7.00 pm The Ski Instructor heads home for a bath and change before the evening really begins – not that he has any plans at the moment but something always develops. As he rounds a corner, a familiar silver Porsche draws up ahead of him; from it steps a stunning woman oozing glamour, self-assurance and wealth. She looks round, then heads purposefully up the street in the direction, as the Ski Instructor immediately realises, of Jean-Pierre's flat . . . The Ski Instructor wastes no time: this is an emergency. In the third bar he checks, there is Jean-Pierre with, as the Ski Instructor had guessed, Caroline; their heads are close together. There is no time for the niceties; the Ski Instructor mutters merely 'Madeleine's here' into his friend's ear. Jean-Pierre, paling momentarily under his tan, springs up and rushes out into the night; Madeleine is, to say the least, very pro-

10.00 pm The Ski Instructor is sipping a cup of coffee in the company of Madeleine and Jean-Pierre – both have suddenly appeared as he finished his dinner and declared themselves ravenous. Caroline is safely out of the way: at five to eight she disappeared for chalet dinner. The Ski Instructor looks across at his companions, sitting close together in a languid, satisfied silence. A strange feeling envelops him; after a few moments he identifies it as a mixture of dissatisfaction and jealousy – no, envy, he thinks hastily. The Ski Instructor is conscious of something he never thought would happen: he has become bored with

Opening gambits (from anyone to anyone).

- Shall we share this chair lift?
- Is the run down to Lachaux open?
- What's the snow like there?
- Is this a black or red run?
- Is there a restaurant at the top?
- What time do the lifts close tonight?
- Which chalet are you staying at?
- It'll be freezing up there – have a nip of cognac?

potting punters like rabbits. Besides, his real passion is skiing, and nothing is worse than going skiing with a girl friend who, like most punters, isn't good enough to keep up with him. It is time, he thinks, to establish a more regular relationship, with a girl whose skiing standard is high, and who will be there at the end of a fortnight. Unaware that he is going through the equivalent of the Ski Instructor's mid-life crisis, his thoughts turn towards the resort's two or three attractive women ski instructors. Who, of course, know all the games ski instructors get up to.

The Ski Bum

Ski bums are people who live to ski, so obsessed by their chosen sport they will do almost anything to pursue it. Most are male Australians or Canadians who mark time the rest of the year as lifeguards, lumberjacks or swimming instructors (though in Verbier even the ski bums are upmarket).

In the resorts, ski bums earn their daily *croûte* by doing a croissant round early in the morning, or working late into the night waxing, filling in or repairing skis. If nothing else offers, they will do washing up or bar work, though the midday shift rather interferes with their skiing. Ski bums live in basements no one else wants, or in hotels and chalets in return for the work they do. Better-off ski bums have caravans (*wagons neige*) and some lodge with a local family.

In many ways ski bums are the equivalent of the Californian beach boy or surfer: bronzed, fit, and glamorous because of their skill and the setting in which they are found. In the old days, ski bums used to do a lot of ski teaching, but now the law is much stricter and schools don't allow it. Much though the ski bum would enjoy this way of earning money, he certainly isn't going to risk having his lift pass taken away, or being skied off a mountain and into a broken leg by some French instructor.

On a high mountainside it is essential to remember where you have parked your skis.

No sensible girl goes out without her earmuffs.

The Chalet Girl

Chalet girls are an entirely British invention: many have 'made in Fulham' stamped right through them (and *that's* no word of a lie). Other nations are understandably suspicious, especially when they hear how little chalet girls are paid. Chalet girls themselves don't complain about their wages: for anyone who thinks cooking is quite fun, chalet work provides a winter in the snow and ideal husband-hunting territory. Indeed, the reason 18-year-olds get turned down for chalet work is not because chalet companies doubt their cooking skills (they don't); what's in question is their ability to handle undesirable passes.

For most punters, trying to have an affair with a chalet girl is about as profitable as spitting into the wind – precious little chance of success and it may all blow back into your face. Not only do chalet girls know what's coming, they invariably share rooms, usually in the cramped cellars of their chalets. Punters, too, have to share rooms; and as all the walls are paper thin chalet girls usually learn what the punters are planning well in advance.

Punter's excuses for tapping on the Chalet Girl's door late at night

——— • ———

- You couldn't be an angel and wake me early – I have to catch the first lift.

——— • ———

- I've got a message for you from your friend.

——— • ———

- I've got rather a headache – I suppose you haven't got a Disprin?

——— • ———

- I've got that book you said you wanted to borrow. I thought you might like to read a bit before you went to sleep.

——— • ———

- D'you feel like coming out for a nightcap? Or we could have one from this bottle I've got here.

——— • ———

- Oh, is *this* your room?

THE WAY TO A CHALET GIRL'S HEART

——— • ———

What Chalet Girls like is friendliness, consideration and the sort of present you can't get in the Alps – Marmite, Mars Bars, the latest glossy magazines. Four things *not* to say to the Chalet Girl are:

- 'But it said in the brochure . . .'
- 'Last year in Courchevel . . .'
- 'Could I have a packed lunch every day, please.'
- 'Do you go with the chalet, Hah, Hah, Hah.'

Sometimes our old friend the altitude gets to chalet girls and they run spectacularly off the rails, allowing themselves to be lured away by ski bums who live in *wagons neige* and leaving messages for the punters that read at first 'Meal in oven', then 'Food in fridge'.

Some chalet girls wind up with a local boy friend, either a ski instructor or the best-looking of the ski bums, hence the curious ménages that spring up all over Parsons Green every April when the chalet girl returns to her guernseys-and-pearls Sloane existence, trailing with her some enormous Canadian or Australian who never opens a book and is only happy when talking about sport. But though some chalet girls go out with the idea of who can have the most men – two from *Supertravel* once kept a check list behind the pantry door – most have their eye on a more enduring relationship, i.e. with a punter.

Chalet girls prefer mixed groups (clued-up female punters only go out in groups where there are extra men to make up for the ones lost to the chalet girls) rather than all-male parties who tend to drink too much – all the mugs get broken, the carefully-prepared dinner is ruined because they

Chalet Girl's excuse for herself

I'm sorry, we're not allowed to fraternise – we lose our jobs.

Chalet Girl's excuse for her friend

She's badly in love with someone in England, and he's coming out next week.

stay in bars drinking until 9.00 pm, and when someone shouts 'Round the Chalet!' they all drop everything and tear round it (last one buys all the Nacs next day). Chalet girls often think if they hear another joke involving the word 'piste' they will throw up.

When boy meets chalet girl most of the love affair is conducted by telephone (one reason chalet girls prefer Swiss, French or Austrian resorts to being at the mercies of the Italian telephone system). Chalet girls think that if one of their male guests writes once, that's nice, twice means interest and three times is serious. Even more so is a punter who's stayed with them in January and books another week in the same chalet in March. Chalet girls have a very high marriage rate – Chalet girls are NICE.

5 Love on the Water

The chief characteristic of love on the water is the contrast between the frequently sordid conditions that surround the reality and the intense glamour of the idea. Quite apart from the subliminal picture of Bing Crosby singing *True Love* to Grace Kelly as the boat scuds along against a backdrop of sparkling sea, blue sky and puffy white clouds, there is the sense of solitude, wonder, freedom, innocence. Sit on a boat with a glass of wine in your hand, phosphorescence glittering on the black wavelets lapping its side and the moon beaming

Anyone with docksiders is halfway there.

pathways across the water, and so potent is the magic that it hardly matters what the man or woman beside you looks like. Surrounded by the beauty of Nature, who are you to defy Nature's most powerful force?

Then there is the boat itself; an escape bubble from ordinary life, it automatically lends itself to the idea of naughtiness, if not of love. Besides, it's so small – how can the two of you *avoid* bumping into each other almost all the time? There is also a more subtle psychological element, summed up by the words of the old song 'Once aboard the lugger and the girl is mine' and exploited to the full by the predatory males sailing seems to throw up in such numbers. 'The moment she steps down the gang-plank, it's the equivalent of taking her to Paris' is one summing up. 'Plus, it's your territory – and she's come into it voluntarily.' Add in the erotic symbolism with which the immediate environment is loaded – the taut curve of the sails, the upright, phallic mast, the straining rigging, the gentle rocking movement – and it's small

position of knowing somebody physically far too well to fancy them – one respected school of thought believes it essential to get the love object back on shore and cleaned up before even considering this aspect of things.

For women, the other great stumbling block is the weather. As it deteriorates and everything, including the person, becomes wet and streaming, men often look better whereas women invariably look worse. Fatigue, strain and concentration combine to give a man in a heavy gale something of the air of a hero in one of the old war films, whereas few women look good with red-rimmed eyes and hair plastered to the skull. This has the knock-on effect of making the man even more short-tempered than usual with his female companion when tiredness drives her to do something not very bright. All in all, love on the water must be fairly robust to survive.

OH, LONELY HEART!

It is perfectly possible to start a sailing career by putting a small-ad in *Yachting Monthly,* but those serious about the sport itself should throw away all the letters which begin 'I am 32, divorced, blue-eyed and have all my own teeth' and answer only those which say 'My boat is 32 foot long with a blue hull, all its original rigging and only one owner.'

Advertisements from Yachting Monthly

Woman, 48, enjoys sailing, windsurfing, skiing, gardening, etc, would like to meet intelligent good-tempered man.

Lady sailing companion required, 40–50, weekends, holidays experience preferred. 30ft yacht, unattached owner.

Pretty sealoving lady would like to sail Solent weekends. Alas no yacht.

Professional woman, experienced sailor, forties, versatile, attractive, good with people, resident London, seeks berth on well-run, wifeless boat.

wonder that many lose all element of control once they have left dry land.

On the other hand, it is impossible to over-emphasise the physical sordidness of small boats and close quarters. After the first day on a comparatively strenuous 24-hour passage on a small boat two comparative strangers are going to know as much about each other's socks, knickers, armpits and rate of beard growth as only happens on dry land after months or even years. Sometimes this leads to the bizarre

Hands on ... deck

Fleeting liaisons, however, are commonplace. Often these are between temporary bachelors (many wives either don't sail or give the whole thing up when they become pregnant or childbound) and the girls who crew, cook on the big yachts, staff local wine bars during the summer season and generally hang around marinas. One common gambit is invite the entire female/young/attractive staff out to the boat after their bar has closed for the night (so is dropping off a load of girls half an hour

PROMISES, PROMISES ...

—————————— *Greater love hath* ——————————
no man ...

Many men are quite unprincipled in their search for free labour to keep their beloved (the boat, that is) in the style to which she is accustomed. As the end of the season approaches, they become increasingly desperate, flinging promises of eternal love and offers of marriage around in wild abandon until some bemused female finally succumbs. Next thing she knows, she is lying flat on her back with, alas, only the bottom of the boat and a brushful of anti-foul above her.

before the wives and children arrive on Saturday morning). After a particularly full-blooded evening ('come for a cruise – we'll have a party') girls are sometimes deposited absentmindedly at a different marina or harbour, often at 5.00 am because of the exigencies of the tide, and have to find their own way back. Men planning to invite girls aboard have to beware of one curious natural phenomenon: very young girls look much older when wearing a bikini than when fully dressed. 'And what do you do, my dear?' shouted one yottie during the preliminary badinage aboard to a full-figured beauty splashing merrily in the water nearby. 'Not much at the moment' she replied, 'but I'm taking my O levels next year'.

What happens where

The smarter marinas and resorts are famous for wife-swapping among the sailing crowd that frequents them; often this takes place on the sort of yacht with so many bowls of gladioli in its stern that clearly it never puts to sea. Sometimes these line the more expensive quays in serried ranks like a series of gently-rocking *Dunroamins* behind whose lace curtains *anything* could be going on. And probably is.

The kind of yacht so vast that helicopters come out of its bows and the doorknobs in the saloon sparkle because they are studded with diamonds is famous for a lot of high class or at least monied adultery. This takes place sometimes between those whose posi-

tion requires them to preserve an unblemished public façade (this kind can be spotted because of the high wages paid to the crew in order to keep their mouths shut) and those who think this is one of the more

—————————
There is an old legend that you can tell when two people in a boat are up to no good because you can see the masts shaking; but with keel boats this doesn't really happen. A far more reliable sign is when a couple emerge during normal daylight hours *blinking at the light*.
—————————

pleasing fruits of money and/or success. The second kind tends to take place in an atmosphere where the paintings come from Christie's, champagne is permanently on tap, and glamorous women to strew around the sun deck are an obligatory part of the

—————————
Before setting off for an afternoon's dalliance, always check that the self-steering is working.
OLD SAILING PROVERB
—————————

furnishings but is otherwise unaesthetic – to be rich enough to be an owner, you have usually left your sexually alluring years a long way behind you. These floating palaces move along the coast from Antibes to Cannes (for the Film Festival) to Monte Carlo for the Grand Prix and allied festivities through the Riviera ports, picking up talent on the way, until they finally reach Greece. Once safely past Paxos, they can let their

watched someone spend the whole winter glueing a few planks together, is now prepared to get in the result herself and actually put to sea?

Yotties

This category of sailing people is basically South-coast-oriented, and dominated by the young and single, many of whom use the parental cottage near Poole Harbour or on the Hamble as their weekend base. Most work in London during the week, the men as stockbrokers, solicitors and accountants, the girls as secretaries, cordon bleu cooks

---

Marriages performed by the captain are valid only for the duration of the voyage.

OLD YOTTIE PROVERB

---

and sometimes nurses, always taking ten days of their holiday to work for one or other company at the Boat Show (pleasuredome for all yotties). This pays off in invitations to crew at weekends, during the various regatta weeks, and of course Cowes Week in August, when 9,000 yotties descend *en masse* on the Isle of Wight.

Male yotties wear jeans, a filthy old shirt, yachting tie and well-cut reefer jacket.

> ❧❧ *Unsuspecting wives don woolly hat and Sunday-Times-offer oilskins to watch the launch off the back of their Vauxhall Viva* ❧❧

Some Yotties find themselves welcome even when the yacht won't be leaving the harbour.

hair down in the privacy afforded by the lonely coves still found in the Ionian isles (though now that sailing is becoming ever more popular some of the cognoscenti are opting for the Asian coast of Turkey).

At the other end of the scale are the owners who build amazing contraptions in the garage from a kit sent by post, persuading their unsuspecting wives to don woolly hat and Sunday-Times-offer oilskins to watch the launch off the back of their Vauxhall Viva. These too are a tribute to passion in their own way: what greater love can there be than that of the wife who, having

The only trouble with windsurfers is that they don't hold two.

For the intelligent male yottie, clothes can serve as a peripheral early warning signal: a quick once-over of the female yottie's attire is as good a way as any of rating his chances. Shoes are the biggest giveway. As one experienced male yottie sums up: 'If she's wearing the wrong kind then you know she's probably not used to the concept of short-term liaisons while at sea. But if she's wearing sloppy old docksiders she's seen and probably done it all before and anything you have in mind won't come as a surprise.'

Pearls and make-up are also indicators; in this case that she may want the affair to last longer the usual brief yottie encounter. When two yotties marry, both go on sailing because the female knows exactly how male yotties behave when on their own and on the loose. All girl yotties are taught in their cradles that a white flag with a cross on it means 'Please come to my assistance'.

The learning factor

Thanks to the boom in sailing over recent years (the Royal Yachting Association's membership is currently increasing at a rate of 10 per cent a year) learner sailors are common. Usually, like many kinds of waterfowl, they are found in pairs, with the male

Female yotties wear oilskins, jeans or, whenever the weather is good enough, shorts (girls with really good figures take up windsurfing) and can be recognised by their calloused hands, healthy-to-weatherbeaten complexions, appallingly foul language and matter-of-fact randiness.

performing a ritual mating dance known as 'teaching her to sail' in front of his reluctant, eager, terrified or sullen female.

For at sea a strange metamorphosis comes over men who haven't previously been nearer any water other than that found in taps. It takes the form of an instant attack of gungho mentality, the barking-out of orders and an all-round skipperliness.

🎔Not THAT bloody rope!🎔

Women from the placider suburbs, who cannot always see the point of suddenly using new words like sole for floor or locker for cupboard, often get rather ratty at the constant correction by the skipper while at the same time feeling rather isolated from the outside world. Hence the scene that you can see enacted at any south coast marina on more or less any day in the season: a man, purple in the face, at the helm of some boat roaring 'Not THAT bloody rope!' while the woman, making desperate attempts to cope, shouts back 'Shut UP, darling, I'm doing my bloody best!' These charming vignettes are interrupted only by the sound of the occasional splash as some woman with more spirit than the rest dives overboard and swims for shore, shouting as she does so 'Right, you sort it out then!'

How dinghy sailors do it

Like ducks, who can only copulate in running water, dinghy sailors seem to need a certain degree of dampness in order to work up a head of steam. The reason for this is that dampness is the dinghy sailor's natural medium. Though wonderfully exhilarating (when you are the right age) dinghy sailing is cold, wet and fiendishly uncomfortable – in short, it is about as anaphrodisiac as a sport can get. The clothes are designed to look hideously unattractive on all save the youngest, slimmest and most stunning of women; and as a preparation for a night of love, the clubs could have been designed by the great Malthus himself. Shower rooms are a jumble of wet clothes on ancient lino floors, the basins are cracked, with hair in the plugholes, a smell of mouldy wetsuits emanates from the cupboards, the small mirrors are carefully sited to give an uninterrupted view of the navel, and the towel left fresh and dry on a hook has somehow fallen off to become sodden and grubby under passing feet. The final *coup de grâce* to any attempt to achieve glamour is given when the newly clean, dry and presentable dinghy sailor finds too late that everywhere he or she sits down to drink a welcome pint has a light coating of salt water from those who have not bothered to change.

Nevertheless, nothing puts off dinghy sailors, who can be found glued together after the sailing club hop in damp and uncomfortable heaps in the bottoms of their dinghies, behind the sail shed or among the sand dunes.

Bunking up

If both parties are experienced sailors, the element of surprise that often forms such a successful part of shore-based seductions is almost invariably absent, if only because of the sheer effort involved in creating a double bunk on a boat. By the time the man has pulled levers, lowered the cabin table, infilled the missing bit with a cushion, and generally gone through all the motions necessary to turn a compact dinette probably already laid for lunch into a love nest,

LOVE IN A COLD – NAY, AN ICY – CLIMATE

Cold is a factor that should never be underestimated in the average sailing liaison. Sailing people must be among the very few who actually make love wearing Norwegian fishing sweaters and oilskins, not from any fetishistic quirk but because it's simply too cold to take them off. Even in the so-called warm months, sleeping in thermal underwear is routine and windsurfers in particular have an awful time getting out of their wet suits when passion seizes them. What with the various layers of latex, oiled wool and proofed canvas that the sailing fraternity have to remove to allow even the necessary minimum of exposure, it takes a certain amount of grit and determination to be bothered at all. No wonder that what female yotties traditionally lie back and think of is the warmer parts of the Empire.

the spontaneity and romance of the moment is irretrievably damaged. Yet if he prepares the bunk before inviting the object of his passion aboard, any yottie girl coming into the cabin will realise at once what he has in mind. One way and another, mystery gets a poor showing at sea.

Sometimes would-be lovers take refuge in the fo'c's'le, often fitted with a double bunk of sorts; but as this is apt to be low, uncomfortable and full of wet and dirty oars, reverberating by day with the thump of feet of those crossing over your boat's foredeck to go ashore, and a hazard at night when drunks fall through because someone

has left the forehatch open, most yotties regard it as a last resort. But the real reason love in a marina is so unromantic is because the marina staff are constantly stumping about asking for harbour dues or coming to moan about your electricity wire – and the thought that you might be otherwise engaged certainly isn't going to inhibit *them*.

Making it

Nowhere is the democracy of the sea more evident than in the Mediterranean. Any good-looking girl in her early twenties possessed of nothing more than an innate sense of style and the urge to be a rich man's plaything can quickly find herself rubbing shoulders with the monied and famous aboard one of the more glamorous yachts that litter the Riviera littoral. There is, of course, a snag: the owners of such boats tend to be old and ugly. Never mind, the more pot-bellied and wrinkled he is, the more anxious he will be to surround himself with nubile and glamorous women in order to impress others by the type of girl he is still able to attract (and with luck, the more likely he is to be impotent).

Starter kit for the grand-yacht groupie is minimal: a few expensive bikinis of the type for which bikini-waxing on a massive scale is necessary, this year's shape in dark glasses, one or two bits of jewellery that don't come apart in the water and an all-over tan (yacht groupies *never* burn). Useful extra skills are fluency in the local language and proficiency at tennis, windsurfing or waterskiing: few *nouveau riche* managing directors, whose idea of *le highlife* is based on Martini commercials, can resist a girl who arrives at the edge of the bar on a monoski and steps ashore dry.

Getting away with it

A boat is one of the safest places in the world for an illicit weekend. There is

HAVE I EVER TOLD YOU, LUCINDA, THAT YOU HAVE A DAMNED ATTRACTIVE BODY?

nowhere more un-interruptable, and isolated, than a boat without radio telephone surrounded by water. In fact, there is only one hazard: if you *are* caught, you are caught in spades. While there are possible reasons for being seen sauntering across the foyer of a large hotel with a married member of the opposite sex, there is only one for the same propinquity in a boat. Hence the old yachting maxim: 'Never let her up on deck until you're at least five miles out at sea'.

Getting it together

Arranging a seduction afloat can be extraordinarily complicated. Even the sailing equivalent of running out of petrol in a dark lane – going aground on a sandbank – is fraught with difficulties: not only must any *rapprochement* be performed at an ever-increasing angle as the boat sags steadily sideways but at the crucial moment the tide may well turn, hurling both of you out of the bunk in a tangled and painful heap. As for the idea of a romantic afternoon's sailing with the loved one, culminating in mooring in some lonely and idyllic spot, there to spend a passionate night rocked by the gently lapping water, planning for this requires a facility for computerlike juggling with a whole series of imponderables. Will the time of the loved one's arrival by train mesh with the tide? Is the wind direction

SEDUCTION AFLOAT

If an overnight stay in France has been particularly successful, the owner of a boat may wish to persuade his lady guest to prolong it. Here are some foolproof reasons for staying on the other side of the Channel.

- I don't like the look of the chart.

- We've missed the tide.

- I think that depression is moving in faster than they thought.

- I'm worried about that chainplate – we'll have the mast down if we try and get back tonight.

- There's been a cock-up with Customs. We have to stay 24 hours while the paperwork goes to Paris.

Here are some excuses for staying out at sea until the love object is thoroughly softened up.

★ We'll never get into Weymouth in this weather.

★ The tide's wrong.

★ We can't sail in that direction, and I'm afraid the engine's failed.

★ For the safety of the ship, we have to continue.

★ More ships have been lost in the entrance to Portland Harbour than anywhere else in the world.

right for dinner at the romantic restaurant down the coast at which a table has been reserved with difficulty? If it begins to rain and after you have finally found the lamp, filled it with paraffin and dug out the matches, will it refuse to light because the match heads are damp and keep flying off? Will the anchor drag in the night, so that both of you have to leave your warm bed at 4.00 am, to come up on deck and drag up 40 yards of slimy chain? And even if everything goes beautifully, will his hat blow overboard next morning in a sudden gust and will she, in trying to get it back, lose his brand-new boathook, thus setting him back £25 and incidentally putting a slight strain on the relationship? It is seldom that this type of thing happens during a night out at the Ritz.

The Royal Yacht Squadron

In many ways the maritime equivalent of Boodles, members of the Squadron are born rather than elected. So passionately do social-climbing yachtsmen desire to storm the ramparts of the Castle that those who have been blackballed during the Squadron's arcane membership process have been known to leave the country and settle for a life of dinghy-sailing in Australia. The Royal Yacht Squadron Ball on the Monday

of Cowes week is attended by all the sailing members of the Royal Family. The club itself has held the Royal Warrant since 1829, has the privilege of flying the White Ensign, and generally dominates the Solent. It only remains to add that despite its treatment of women as a separate and inferior species (not allowed in the Members' dining room, for example), members of the Royal Yacht Squadron *always* get their girl.

Racing crews

While yachting people in general drink a fair amount and some yachting people drink far more than a fair amount, most ocean racers these days are dry. In high-performance competitive sailing, you don't risk several hundred thousand pounds' worth of boat for a few drinks. It is rather the same with love.

Aboard racing yachts, emotional entanglements are firmly discouraged. In any case, as racing crews have to be large and tough, only the occasional woman is allowed on board, usually as cook or navigator. The result is that racing crews go ashore looking glamorous and heroic in search of the local talent, which they are then unable to bring back to the boat because all the berths will be occupied by the other half of the crew catching up on its sleep (racing crews commonly double up).

Racing crews are the ones seen wandering round Deauville bashing their heads against walls.

Flotilla holidays

The erotic possibilities of the flotilla holiday – hot sun, some gentle sailing, meals with litres of rough red wine at local tavernas, barbecues on Greek beaches under the stars – often come to naught because of one of the least pleasant of human instincts: the urge to dominate. The men vie as to who is going to be skipper, showing off in front of the women and smiling through gritted teeth at each other; the women do the same thing but far less obviously, battling it out as to who takes control of the shopping, who can produce a cordon bleu repast out of two sardine tails and an unripe fig. Even worse, amorous pursuit and eventual success become common knowledge throughout the entire flotilla instantly – in a boat, you can hear *everything*.

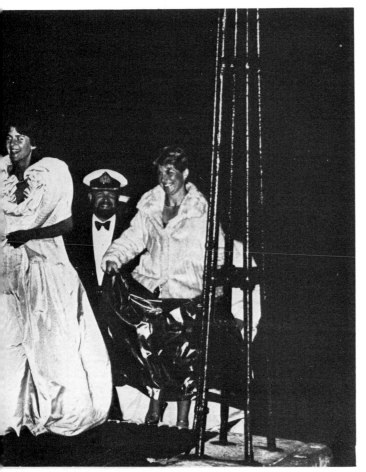

Arriving at the Royal Yacht Squadron Ball, Cowes.

6 Love in the Hunting Field

Not for nothing are foxhounds so often divided into Dog Pack and Bitch Pack, and hunted on different days. Everyone knows what would happen on idle moments if they were out together.

It is rather the same with those who follow them. One reason affairs flare up so quickly in the hunting field is sheer physical fitness – to ride a six-hour day across country on a horse that pulls like a train for the first hour or so requires peak condition.

Add in propinquity, shared interest in an all-absorbing sport and above all the ever-present risk of danger and it hardly seems surprising that the adrenalin sloshing around all day should produce an extra-ordinarily high level of sexual activity as soon as the winter twilight falls.

Much of the more picturesque aspect of this subsidiary sport is, alas, no more. Gone are the days when one noted hunting buck kept a mistress for several summer weeks in

Everyone out hunting always dresses to kill.

a spinney near Melton. 'She slept on a lilo and every day McDougal would ride out and bring her caviar and smoked salmon' is how Simon Blow describes the affair in *Fields Elysian*.

Nevertheless, one thing hasn't changed. Now as then, the distinguishing mark of love in the hunting field is that it is nearly always adulterous.

In part, this is because the young and the single spend most of their weekdays at work (and conducting their romances elsewhere). But the spark that sets the amorous tinder

spouse up to and including a crashing fall is a well-known hunting trait – but because of your horses. Those of a married couple, accustomed to the constant togetherness of the same field and stables, act like lovesick teenagers – sidling up for a nuzzle at every opportunity, attempting to gallop or jump together, and finding each other like balls of mercury whenever they have been separated. Sometimes lovers who have been exercising together regularly but illicitly have the game given away like this by their horses.

OPENING GAMBITS

Best of all is everyone's favourite compliment, '*Didn't* you go well!'; others are offering a drink of brandy from your hip flask or – in hunts like the Quorn, full of people who roar up the M1 in their Mercedes – a lift back to London. Jumping off to do up a fetlock boot that's come undone, rebuckling a strap or simply holding open a gate at a strategic moment also work well.

Women with their eye on the Master ring him up in the early summer and say in excited tones, 'I've got a litter!' (no hunting person needs to specify which member of the animal kingdom has just given birth). He is round in a flash ... and off the two of you go, down the lush verges and along sweet-smelling hedgerows. So many and varied are the excuses for a visit – you think the vixen has moved her cubs or a badger has joined them – that not infrequently ladies who use this one wind up with a litter of their own.

ablaze is usually opportunity: while in hunting's heartland, Leicestershire, there are plenty of hunting couples, it is a curious fact that around Britain generally it is usually either husband or wife who follows hounds – but seldom both.

The reasons for this vary from marrying a non-hunting partner to one or other giving it up for reasons ranging from childbirth to a dislocated back. And occasionally, too, one half of a couple who have never taken any exercise more violent than gardening will suddenly spring into the saddle – Gloucestershire in particular is famous for late starters.

Naturally, this allows considerable freedom – having a husband or wife out with you in the hunting field is as good as a chastity belt. Not for any obvious reason – ignoring the behaviour or difficulties of your

So those who are planning an affair aim to have got it off the ground well in time for the Opening Meet. (Hunting people measure their year from this marker point, usually the first Saturday in November; other vital dates are the point-to-point – somewhere between February and May but always the same Saturday each year – and the Hunt Ball. Hunter trials are slotted in

> **❦❦** *She slept on a lilo and every day McDougal would ride out and bring her smoked salmon* **❦❦**

spring or autumn, and the Master's diary is ringed throughout the summer with Puppy Shows.) Nor does anyone want their tentative opening moves watched by eyes trained not to miss a flicker of bracken as a fox is about to break cover and therefore more than capable of spotting what is going on between two of the riders at their side.

Nevertheless, plenty can go on. There

> ❦❦ *Fortunately most horseboxes not only lock but are plentifully supplied with rugs* ❦❦

are assignations to be made – hunting, like other risk sports, is fraught with danger to stay-at-home spouses – and images to be established.

For men, there are endless opportunities to show off to the female of their choice. Being terribly brave and jumping bigger fences than anyone else is one way of showing how mucho macho you are; another is by riding the sort of difficult horse for which sheer brute strength is an essential prerequisite. Women can use this one in reverse, by saying how frightened they are of their horse and getting the man to ride it; unless you ride sidesaddle, swapping horses is rapidly done during even the briefest pause. This ploy also has the merit of providing the perfect excuse for meeting again at the end of the day.

An even more surefire way of manoeuvring a meeting is each to park your horsebox near the other's (by prior arrangement, of course). Just as it is routine to take a flask of coffee or sloe gin and perhaps a bar of chocolate or a couple of sandwiches along, so no homebound spouse could possibly object to your spending half an hour or so eating them in company of a few friends

– well, one, but who's counting? – at the end of the day. Fortunately, most horseboxes not only lock but are plentifully supplied with rugs. The best of these by common consent is the Lavenham, a weatherproof, highly insulated quilted affair rather like a light duvet – and frequently used as one.

When to start a love affair

The best time to launch any kind of love affair is early on in the cubhunting season: since so much of cubhunting involves simply standing around there is plenty of time for the tricky beginning stages when a certain amount of talk and mutual self-revelation between the parties is necessary.

Weather conditions are often perfect – many September mornings start symbolically with an exciting tingle that promises later warmth – and there is even the

chance of privacy: with luck, the pair of you may have been sent around the other side of a covert by the Master to stop the cubs emerging. And there you stand, as the dew dries on the grass, with plenty of time for all those refinements like lowered lashes and the quickly averted gaze. (Non-hunting people's standby, body language, is necessarily restricted in the hunting field: if you use it too expressively, your horse may take fright. Hence, of course, Mrs Patrick Campbell's famous dictum: 'Doesn't matter what you do, as long as you don't frighten the horses'.)

But although by 10.30 in the morning it is perfect dallying weather, only the brave or the desperate will get off their horses and hook the reins over a handy branch – at any moment the huntsman could come galloping down a ride.

So varied is the average hunting field that only two or three of its characters emerge with any kind of distinctive sexual profile. The first is a particular kind of predatory woman with whom few men are safe – fortunately for civilisation as we know it, the welfare of her horse comes far and away first, so that a well-timed distraction – 'Isn't he going a bit short on the near fore, Vanessa?' – nearly always works. Daddy tended to be a key figure in the lives of these ladies;

> **❝** *Body language, is necessarily restricted in the hunting field: if you use it too expressively your horse may take fright* **❞**

alternatively, hunting daddies frequently produce a breed of Amazons – at the extreme end of the spectrum they tend to be mannish rather than devouring.

The Master

The sun around whom these women revolve and prime sexual target for the entire female portion of the field is the Master. Some Masters are hound men, some riding men, and some ladies' men, but all are anointed with the irresistible aphrodisiac of complete power. The ruthlessness that so many possess only adds to their charm; it should also be noted that the better a Master is at his job, the more noticeable and effective his appeal.

Because being a Master means having a sizeable private income, one familiar stereotype is the young and goodlooking amateur dedicated to his profession since the days when an expensive education meant singlemindedly following the Eton Beagles (of which he naturally became Master at the earliest possible age); but unable actually to hunt hounds until he finds a wife rich enough to support him. Usually, he settles this pressing need as briskly as possible, his choice falling on either a rich manufacturer's daughter dazzled by the glamour of the whole horse world, or the hunting daughter of some neighbouring landowner, depending on which appears first.

But to his admirers, marriage is no bar. And curiously enough, even if they met in the hunting field, the Master's wife often

ends by giving up hunting. Sometimes this is because of repeated pregnancies ('Celia's breeding again'), sometimes through going on the bottle, a condition often caused by the agony of seeing so many other women chase her husband. Nevertheless, she still continues to subsidise him, knowing that while she enables him to pursue his main passion in life he will never leave her. Wise Masters' wives stick closely to the old adage *Out of Sight, Out of Mind* (or as their husbands would put it *Out of Scent, Out of Mind);* only when a female rival not only

---

RHYME OF THE
ANCIENT FOXHUNTER

'The older I get, as the years go by,
And I totter towards the tomb,
I find myself caring less and less,
About who goes to bed with whom.'

(This exquisite verse was penned by the noted foxhunter Sir Harry Llewellyn, coincidentally at the height of the publicity about his sons Dai and Roddy.)

---

amorous but considerably richer heaves into view, do they begin to worry.

Lady Masters are not so often sex objects in the same way. This is partly because they take their duties very seriously, partly because by the time they become Masters they are usually fairly well on in years – 'weathered' is an adjective that frequently springs to mind. When a lady Master is young and beautiful, her whole life sometimes appears to be devoted either to the chase or avoiding capture herself, and if she has a male Joint Master(s) she is automatically assumed to be having an affair with one if not all, rather in the way actresses are conventionally supposed to have a fling with their leading man for the duration of play.

Women who are in love with the Master will bribe the Field Master (in any way open to them) to send them to stand at the corner of a covert, which carries with it the privi-

lege of riding with the whippers-in and the beloved object himself instead of with the rest of the field. The grinding of teeth when some lucky female follower is given the good news with the words 'Go and take a view' can be heard in the next-door hunt's Tuesday country.

But moral danger is not the only one a popular Master has to face. His tougher lady admirers ride so close to him they can damage not only his horse but sometimes hounds. If this happens they are castigated in scathing language to which they dare not answer back, and move away looking desperate until they have regained control (the ultimate sanction is to be sent home, which reduces even strong men to tears); nevertheless, on the rare occasions when the Master takes a fall they fight to cradle his head in their arms. It is not surprising that in more than one hunt the features of the younger followers have been noted to bear a strong resemblance to those of the Master.

Girl grooms

These occupy a somewhat ambivalent position in the amatory lexicon of the foxhunter. You have sex with girl grooms – having a go in the horsebox is considered quite dashing – but not affairs; on the other hand, you sometimes marry them. Thus, on the rare occasions when affairs do take place, they are kept quite secret until the couple run off together. Even this is a bolt not only into the blue but from the blue: by putting forward the first feed of the day (no girl groom

RIPPING FETLOCKS MISS PENDLETON

THE HUNT BALL

If Hunt Balls did not exist, would it be necessary to invent them? Yes. YES. By January, when most of these saturnalia take place, muscles and libidos have been tuned to peak condition; and the faint but unmistakable tang of Misrule still lingers in the air. *Something* has to give.

So much has been written about Hunt Balls – the sexual high jinks, the unflagging abandon, the glamour of the male hunting person in his colourful evening finery, the eruption of animal spirits underscored by sporadic, urgent blasts on hunting horns – that it only remains to note one point. Is the venue a public building, such as town hall, or private house? One means coke in the lavatories, the other – bedrooms.

The Horse and Hound Ball

worth her pony nuts would leave her charges unfed) she and the erring husband can tiptoe out of the house in stocking feet and be halfway across England by sun-up, with nobody in the house noticing a thing until she fails to turn up for her morning coffee after exercise.

It is not so much that employers think of girl grooms as beyond the pale classwise – many are from far smarter families than the one that pays their wages – but rather that from a husband's point of view, the girl groom is the one female directly under his wife's eyes; also, living in the house, she is taboo – unless both fall victim to true love.

Much more common than the girl groom as love object for the husband is the girl groom as spy or confidante for the wife, or message-taker for either of them. Being caught in the middle of complicated marital crossfire is a far more common cause of the girl groom's departure than unrequited love.

Horse, horse all day long – the saga of Virginia and Timmie

Scene one

Virginia is a goodlooking woman of 38, whose marriage broke up five years ago. She lives in a small but pretty cottage, chosen because of the stables sold with it and the grazing offered by a nearby farmer. Her two sons are at boarding school, paid for by her husband, about whom she seldom speaks (out of the blue he had shouted at her as he left: 'It's horse, horse, horse with you all day long! Why don't you go the whole hog and sleep with the bloody animal?' She had looked back at him with the incomprehension of one for whom horses and hunting are not only a way of life but an all-consuming passion – so much so, in fact, that although she hasn't bothered to think this

ing grass rates near-canonisation in the eyes of most Masters of Foxhounds).

Unobtrusively she urges her horse, Guardsman, nearer Timmie's as they trot along a narrow lane to the wood 300 yards off. Later in the season, they could have been drawing a field of kale, with no chance of finding anything except a fox. As it is, by the time they reach this sizeable copse, Virginia's horse is close behind his; Virginia has already worked out that the experienced Timmie, along with those riders close to him, will probably be sent round to the other side to stop the cubs slipping out.

Luck is on Virginia's side. She and Timmie have been sent, alone, to watch a wide gap in the undergrowth edging a little wood.

Soon they are deep in hunting chat. Virginia hangs flatteringly on his every word. Under the black velvet hunting cap her complexion is peachlike, the lavishly-applied blusher (see Costume and Make-up) gives her eyes an added sparkle. While Timmie wonders why he hasn't noticed before how attractive she is, Virginia, edging Guardsman fractionally closer with an invisible squeeze of her left leg, thinks once

out, hunting is now also her only means of social contact).

Today, however, any such thoughts are far away. It is 6.45 on a sparkling mid-September morning, the small field have moved off from the meet at Nether Meynell, and on the way to the first covert she has spotted the broad back of a local horsey glamour-figure. Timmie plays polo, rides in point-to-points, and hunts three days a week; his farm, almost needless to say, is turned over to grazing (good gallop-

GETTING YOUR PRIORITIES RIGHT

Although love is the second most prevalent activity among hunting people, it is never allowed to interfere with the main business of life. During the Season (no, not Ascot and all that, silly, the *proper* one) hunting days are regarded as so sacred that hunting people never have a wedding, christening or indeed any other tribal ritual on them. 'Extraordinary – they've arranged his funeral for Wednesday!' is a common hunting cry when someone with a non-hunting family has been inconsiderate enough to pop off during the precious winter months.

again how glad she is he doesn't kick (coquettish and charming though a red tail bow looks, no serious flirt should ride a horse with an uncertain temper).

As the sun rises, the mists scatter and small droplets of moisture glitter on every branch, the still air hardly disturbed by the crashing and whimpering on the far side of the covert. But this peaceful idyll may come to an end at any moment if hounds find them; Virginia realises she must make a move. 'I wish you'd advise me, Timmie', she says looking up between her lushly-mascaraed lashes (fortunately, her horse is half a hand shorter than Timmie's), 'Guardsman has this terrible habit of always running out to the left at his fences.'

Timmie looks at her thoughtfully. 'He needs to be jumped a few times by someone strong. I could come over and help you school him – how about Wednesday?'

The first kill of the day has been achieved.

Costume & Make-up

In few other areas of life is wearing the correct clothes so central to getting an affair off the ground. The reason is that in any pack with pretensions to smartness – and the smarter, i.e. richer, the pack the greater the number of affairs – you are frowned upon almost to the point of ostracism for wearing the wrong ones, an initial barrier few flirtations can surmount. (The age of the garments in question, however, does not matter: when one famous Master, Lord Daresbury, was asked what he did with his old hunting clothes he replied 'Fold them up and put them on the next morning'.)

These rigid sartorial standards also mean that, just as in Edwardian times and for the same reason, a certain amount of leisure is needed to pursue an affair to its successful conclusion. Hunting clothes are extremely time-consuming to put on or take off, from pulling on boots over silk stockings to

> ## 66 How glad she is he doesn't kick 99

doing up the endless little gold safety pins that hold a hunting tie in position under the coat. Though no woman these days has herself sewn into her riding habit to achieve true form-fitting perfection as did the Empress of Austria when she hunted with the Pytchley a century ago, a good (i.e., tight) fit is still important for boots*, breeches and, to a lesser extent, coat.

One highly noticeable characteristic of hunting women is the incredible amount of make-up they wear, usually enhanced by a black velvet cap (only supposed to be worn by hunt servants, farmers or children but instantly seized on by women as being far more becoming than a bowler). Hunting women claim that the layers of foundation, lipstick and mascara are to protect their skins; a more likely explanation is that when everyone is in the same 'uniform' all messages have to be signalled by the face. So widespread is this phenomenon that at the Centenary Dinner for Masters of Foxhounds the Prince of Wales remarked in his speech that although it was nice to see so many friends 'I don't find it easy to recognise the ladies with so much less make-up on than in the hunting field'. Perfume, however, is strictly taboo: come out reeking of *Femme* and you may be sent home for interfering with hounds. In the hunting field, the only kind of scent permitted belongs to the fox.

* A marvellous leg for a boot' is the ultimate hunting compliment on the male physique.

Virginia and Timmie

Scene two

The affair between Timmie and Virginia is now at full gallop. They are at the stage when neither can bear to be apart for long while remaining fondly confident that no one else has noticed a thing, although the only person still totally unaware of the way the land lies is Timmie's wife Clarissa, by now accustomed to seeing Virginia arrive every day to help exercise Timmie's horses (fortunately, one of the girl grooms has recently left).

After a while Clarissa, quite pleased at having the house to herself again and not uninfluenced by the thought of the wages they are saving, says to Timmie: 'Do we *really* need to look for another girl, darling? Virginia doing the horses in return for you mounting her one day a week seems to work very well. And the great thing is, she very seldom comes in the house.'

The house, however, is about the only place where Virginia doesn't come; and she is certainly mounted more than once a week. Sometimes she and Timmie ride out openly: 'Think we'll exercise together today' says Timmie cheerily (and truthfully). Occasionally one rides while the other drives to a distant field where Timmie has to put up some jumps; this is known as 'getting ready for hunter trials'. On one never-to-be-forgotten day Timmie forgot to put the usual headcollar in the back of the Land Rover and they actually had to practise some jumping.

On hunting days there is little problem. By parking their horseboxes near each other or deciding to go home at the moment of optimum closeness to Virginia's cottage, they can usually snatch 40–90 minutes together. Virginia is rather dreading the onset of summer – the dead season for hunting people from the amatory point of view as well – but with luck a few people will

have started asking them to the same dinner parties.

She has reckoned without Timmie's resourcefulness. Every two or three weeks he tells Clarissa he has to go to a bull show or an agricultural fair, droning on at such boring length about what he is looking for in the way of potential milk sire or chain harrow that when he eventually asks her to come with him to look at another 20

Getting away with it

You can be late home from hunting in exactly the same way you can be late home from the office. Even the excuses have a familiar ring to them.

- 'Timmie had rather a bad fall and I thought I'd see him home.'

- 'Timmie's horse cut itself rather badly on some wire and I said I'd wait with him until the vet came.'

- 'We finished miles away and it took me ages to find the horsebox.'

- 'I got talking to Timmie and that new girl of his – I thought you'd like to hear all about her.'

If you are the Master, you have the best alibi of all: it is your duty not only to stay to the bitter end but frequently to call on some farmer or Hunt supporter on the way home. To be happy when married to a Master means being a modern-day version of Caesar's wife – not so much above suspicion as above suspecting.

Charolais or four acres of heavy machinery ('only three days darling, and I'd like to have you with me') she tells him hastily there is far too much to do in the garden at the moment; Virginia, prepared to let the weeds but not the grass grow under her feet, simply turns the key in her cottage door and whizzes up the M1.

Falling off

Falling off, or 'taking a fall' as it is usually known, is something most hunting people secretly dread. Quite apart from any bruising of the ego (only when your horse's shoulder actually touches the ground can you use the salving phrase 'my horse came down with me'), the list of casualties in any one season is formidable. Some hunting counties are alive with the sound of snapping collarbones and cracking ribs; arms, legs and necks break, people get kicked on the head; being dragged or winding up a paraplegic is the fate everyone justifiably fears most. Yet when hounds are running nobody stops for someone who falls ('Get out of the way!' is a more likely cry) though catching their horse to prevent it from damage is perfectly permissible.

Nevertheless, even falling off can be overlaid – frequently the right word – with amatory implications. Since only newly-weds, lovers or the Prince of Wales (noted for his chivalry) stop for the fallen, hunting wives often check up on their suspicions with a cleverly-timed comment. 'Did you see that girl lying motionless in ditch back there? I'm almost certain it was Virginia' has had many a husband yanking his horse unwillingly round as he mutters 'Someone ought to see to her – you go on'. When a man falls off, he is either ignored completely or approached by two women – the mistress rushing up to help her beloved and the wife anxious to stop her. It is not unknown for blows with a hunting whip to be exchanged on such occasions. 'Fortunately, hunting clothes are very thick and protective' says one mistress who endured such an onslaught.

But even the claims of passion sometimes fail. In the Belvoir, noted as the kamikaze hunt for its tremendous goers, when one beauty noted for her lavishly-distributed favours fell off into a ditch, one of her lovers jumped over her with the cry: 'Alone at last – and for once, not mounted!'

Virginia and Timmie
Scene three

Virginia is cooling off. She has spent as much of the summer as she could following Timmie around to shows and fairs, and she has managed to accompany him to several hunter trials and Events because of her undoubted (by now) knowledge of his horses as well as their owner. But she is rather fed up with the claustrophobic conditions in which their affair is conducted, notably the cramped living quarters of Timmie's horsebox (in the horse world, these vehicles play the part of the notorious caravan on film or TV set). Even the horsebox, however, is better than his Land Rover, their usual resort at the end of the day: it is difficult enough taking hunting clothes off anyway, thinks Virginia, without getting them caught up in the four-wheel drive. She wishes she and Timmie were well-heeled enough to live in a hunting country where

DO come back to tea!

The Hunting Tea – several boiled eggs apiece, lots of buttered toast, very rich fruit cake and surgical dissection of the character and performance of everyone out that day – is a famous institution and therefore a perfectly legitimate reason for being home late. Nevertheless, everyone keeps a very sharp eye out to see who gets invited back to which house at the end of the day.

Apart from the scones and home made strawberry jam, the salient characteristics of the hunt tea is a lot of healthy hunger combined with considerable relief at still being in one piece. This produces an atmosphere in which one thing can and frequently does lead to another. The timid can be helped along by the offer of a hot bath or a little judicious massage for stiff muscles.

All in all, the phrase 'What about a crumpet?' is not one to use lightly at these gatherings.

you automatically had second horses; there, she thinks dreamily, all you have to do is nip back three-quarters of an hour early to change horses . . .

Besides, she has begun to wonder uneasily if Clarissa *knows*. Though she has stuck rigorously to what Timmie calls the *Safe Period* for making telephone calls to him, even this is now dangerous: Clarissa has bought a cordless phone which she carries around everywhere, and Virginia means *everywhere*, like some kind of pet. And recently – the hunting season has started again – she has taken to following hounds in her car, equipped with a pair of binoculars. Who knows what she will spot?

Virginia gives a deep sigh. It is time to part. How can she break it to Timmie in a way that will not only save his face but cause him to think of her with sympathy and approval, while at the same time providing an excuse for a few months' separation?

Her thoughts stray to the fascinating man she met at a tennis party last June (tennis is a great summer game for foxhunting people, frequently giving a new meaning to the expression 'mixed doubles', since being rich enough to hunt also means you can afford your own court). Was not the stranger's conversation spattered with references to deer of all descriptions? And did he not live in Devon? Inspiration comes to her in a flash. 'Timmie' she says, looking at him tenderly as they queue up for a hunt jump in the middle of a barbed-wire fence, 'I think I'm going down to Exmoor for some staghunting next month'.

'I've tried every ploy I know. Will this one come off?'

Hunting proverb

Never trust a girl who wears
black knickers or a man who
hunts South of the Thames

Through the great British public runs a complete sub-culture: those whose chief interest in life is the inward or outward functioning of their own bodies. Some are health food freaks, other running fanatics, but all have one thing in common: they are obsessed with their own bodies, a secret society who recognise each other through here the flash of an E-additive counter, there the opening of an attaché case to reveal shorts and a bullworker.

With body people, you can only see through a class darkly, since their accents, surroundings and way of life matter far less to them than their persons. Body people prefer being best-dressed to best-addressed, and though many of them prefer to wear the sort of ancient exercise kit *real* athletes or dancers wear, when they do take to designer clothes they invariably wear them so that others can see the label (this is known as Yves-dropping).

In the raw

Body people on the make often hunt in pairs (as at health farms); those doing it for themselves tend to be introverted and frequently silent. Though there are basically two kinds of body people: those with the opposite sex in mind – if you've got a good body you can pull – and those doing it for themselves, all of them have one thing in common: they are highly narcissistic – even those maintaining their physique for the one they love are actually looking at it for themselves. Hence the importance of mirrors in the body cult: body people stare constantly at themselves, or each other, in the nearest handy mirror. Top health clubs know this and every wall is lined from floor to ceiling with mirrors. When body people have mirrors on the bedroom ceiling, it is merely to check their stomach muscles during early morning sit-ups.

Courtship for body people has, like the rest of the world, a lot to do with food, but in their case it means sifting out what's bad for them, comparing training régimes, or planning what they're going to eat. Although usually raw, this always takes far longer to prepare than most cooked food. Muesli is concocted ounce by ounce with nuts, rolled oats, dried fruit and bran, fruit juice is lovingly squeezed in a complicated machine that takes hours to clean afterwards, long detours have to be made when shopping to find the necessary skim or goat's milk. Checking that sugar and salt is absent from their food and the coffee is decaffeinated also gives hours of innocent fun; and the truly dedicated ones will tank up on electrolyte drinks to make sure they are ingesting exactly the right amount of body minerals like sodium, potassium, calcium or magnesium.

Looking after the body is such a full time occupation it flows over from food into every aspect of life, from shaping up to sleeping – body people are *fanatic* about sleep, always going to bed at 10.30 sharp whatever they may happen to be doing. When a body person says 'I must go to bed now' in the middle of a passionate embrace, it means *exactly that*. Fortunately, it is only a short step from being obsessed with your own body to being obsessed with someone else's. Like the gym, the health club is one of the world's great meeting places, one of its chief attractions being that you see exactly what you are getting (or in the case of shyer members, hoping to get). For, though marginally more flattering with their concealment of lumps, bumps, stretch marks, cellulite, excess body hair and other blemishes, there is no doubt that leotards are a whole lot more like skin than clothes.

The mating dance

The result of this sudden exposure of the entire physique to the assessing gaze of those around is that body language becomes not only more important, but exaggerated. In health clubs, there is no place for the nuance of the lifted eyebrow when everyone else is working away with the jutting hip.

Thus there is a frenzied sexual symbolism in the posing that goes on before class, men and girls 'displaying' in a stylised ritual reminiscent of those bird courtship dances so often seen in wildlife films.

Girls stand around with pelvis tilted, feet in dancer pose, stomachs and cheeks sucked and bosoms lifted so that the unwary male who comes too close risks having his eye knocked out by a muscular nipple, sometimes varying this statuesque immobility by 'practising a few stretch exercises', notably the ones designed to see how far apart they can open their legs.

Men run frantically on the spot, bending their arms into chicken-wings and jerking them back and forth like a rooster about to crow, or doing endless symbolic press-ups in front of the female they wish to impress. Occasionally, one forgets himself and starts beating his chest.

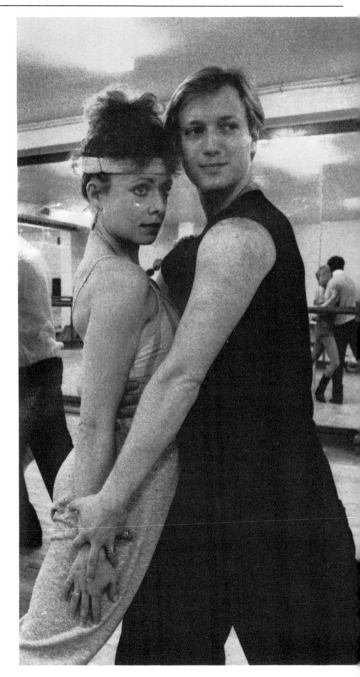

It just takes two to tango.

Sexercise

The whole idea is to show off the three S's – strength and stamina for men, suppleness for women – which are the health club goals and coincidentally equally desirable in bed. Even the exercise equipment and the various classes are designed to reinforce this, with sexual brownie points going to the girl who can perform the classic 'rag doll' exercise – flopping forward so that the *entire trunk* touches the floor while legs point east and west.

In consequence, the key area for men is the upper torso, while women are obsessed with the inner thigh and its environs – indeed, in any health club worthy of the name it is impossible not to be constantly

---

BODY LANGUAGE

- Gosh, what biceps!

———————·———————

- Have you tried the Pogostick?

———————·———————

- Have you tried the PT bouncer?

———————·———————

- My goodness, aren't you doing well – up to E already!

———————·———————

- Your quadriceps are in great shape – been working on them long?

———————·———————

- Would you like to borrow my pedometer?

———————·———————

- Goodness, we've got the same resting pulse rate!

———————·———————

---

conscious of the female crotch, especially as viewed during some of the more explicitly gynaecological exercises.

Once in class and watching both the instructor and themselves in the mirror, a film of narcissism descends on everyone. In the Nautilus room, however, it is a different story. Here, where 90 per cent of anyone's conversation is about their own or someone else's body, a heavy aura of sex hangs almost tangibly in the air, with flashing eyes sending unmistakable messages across the black leather couches. As everyone there knows, if you are physically fit, lovemaking is all the more interesting, and strength, stamina and suppleness can add a whole new dimension to the other S.

Teacher's pet

Those who teach at health clubs have an unrivalled opportunity of checking out the attractiveness rating of their classes. Like ski instructors, they are usually a sexual focus; even so a few trifling preliminaries are usually necessary to cut their prospect out of the herd.

- That's too heavy for you
- Come on, you can pump a bit harder!
- *You* don't look as though you need much toning up
- Your thighs are thinner since last week!
- Why don't you lie down here and I'll check your tummy muscles?
- That leotard's a lovely shape
- You're so fit now you ought to try it with weights
- No, no, no, you bend at the hips like *this.* Try it over my arm.
- If you're interested, I always go for a run on Saturday mornings at 10 o'clock.

Hey, Teach!

Many of the most desirable bodies in health clubs are found among the instructors who are, of course, both male and female. Here are some ways of attracting their attention.

- What should I be concentrating on?
- What make of running shoes do *you* wear?
- Can I buy you an orange juice after class?
- I'm a bit worried about my lats – will you show me some good exercises?
- I don't seem able to fasten this lapstrap.

- Your muscles look so-o hard – may I feel them?
- What would you like for Christmas – lace-on weights, personalised Heavy Hands, or me?

As with any sexual arena, the health club isn't all sweetness and light. With everyone striving for the position of Alpha Male or Female, naked competitiveness frequently shades off into outright rivalry. Here are some useful put-down phrases:

- Call *that* a stretch!
- You ought to try sweating a bit more
- You'd look slimmer if you held your stomach in – oh, you *are* holding it in
- Why haven't I changed? I'm doing the next class as well
- Don't blame *me* if your Achilles tendon goes – those shoes are useless
- *My* resting pulse rate's only 51

Health farms

Health farms are famous for the tremendous amount of free-floating lust in their atmosphere. So unadulterated by feelings

THE HEALTH CLUB JOKE

Where's my dumb-bell?

Oh, here she is.

of emotion or passion is the natural urge towards the opposite sex in many of the ritzier establishments that if there is such a thing as 'pure' lust, it is here, it is here, it is here.

Several factors conspire to produce this high ground level of randiness. The first is that almost as soon as you arrive at a health farm, you have to take all your clothes off, and to the average well-adjusted adult, undressing during the day immediately suggests sex. So does the fact that you stay undressed: most people remain in robes – often surprisingly brief – all day long. As these can be judiciously adjusted to reveal, or even fall open, a consciousness of the possibilities is ever-present. Despite the cry of 'Look out – man about!' or the proffering of towels, women with pretty figures often manage to be stepping naked out of the steam cabinet as a man passes by, before casually picking up their robe and flinging a provocative 'I feel like a massage now' over their shoulder as they saunter off. As for the health farm's equivalent of the bar where you check out new arrivals, the jacuzzi – well, in what other area of life do strangers

Introductions are unnecessary in this alfresco jacuzzi.

meet for the first time wearing only bikinis or less (some jacuzzis are topless), while being massaged in all their most sensitive zones by caressing jets of warm water?

The only deterrent to mass orgies, runs one theory, is the insurmountable fact that many health farm customers are physically unappealing (those who are there for a rest or an enjoyably amorous week, rather than to slim, hoover up most of the talent in the first few days). But thanks to one of Nature's kindlier tricks, after a few days of deprivation even the plumpest fellow-being suddenly seems more attractive. Besides, there is the shared link of food: what you do eat and what you don't.

For food in a health farm takes the place of sex in the ordinary world as a topic of conversation. It is starting point, common bond, forbidden fruit, aphrodisiac and shared password for approaching the opposite sex. Once well into a week where an extra carrot is the highlight of the day, sharing a passion fruit is almost a betrothal ceremony, while the surreptitious offer of a packet of crisps can make the most resilient virtue waver. Sexual interest is shown over a

I HEAR THAT YOU'VE SMUGGLED IN SOME BLACK FOREST GATEAU

precious mid-morning fruit juice, while 'Psst! want to sneak out with me to the pub this evening?' is as erotic as an invitation to a weekend in Paris.

Despite the lack of mobility of many of the participants, health farm affairs take off at lightning speed. Like romance on the ski slopes, both parties know they are only there for a limited period (though in health farms, it's a week rather than a fortnight), so there simply isn't time for the pacing, the gradual breaching of the frontiers of

OPENING GAMBITS

- And why did *you* come here? it wasn't to improve your figure, obviously
- Would you like to join me on a run?
- I know someone in the kitchen who can keep his mouth shut!
- What about a game of tennis?
- You ought to try archery – I'll show you how to hold the bow
- What diet are you on?
- I heard you talking about Monte Carlo – mind if I join your table?
- Your should have been here last Christmas – oh, I could tell you some stories!
- Like a lift to the village?

In the asexual surroundings of the Health Farm dining room, where bright lights beam down on the tables for four, signalling availability while saying nothing that is not socially correct is an important skill. Here are a few favourite methods;

- It's so nice to meet some new friends – with Eric away four nights a week on his engineering trips you can't imagine how lonely it gets.
- She's a marvellous wife, of course, but she's a real homebody – I can't even get her to come out for a drink.
- I brought the Porsche down because it's easier to zip around in.
- Who feels like a feast in the dorm tonight?

NB So strong is the sense of camaraderie that if anyone denigrates a member of the opposite sex, it is a fair bet they have been rejected.

intimacy, that goes on in most affairs. Nor do the conventions and restrictions of the outside world hold good: the bond of the grapefruit overcomes age, religion, culture and class gaps. And while in any Grand Hotel the words 'Would you like to come and have a glass of champagne in my room after lights out?' can mean only one thing, in a health farm it is merely offering the hand of friendship – on an empty stomach, in a boarding school atmosphere, days and hours cease to have their usual meaning. Away from the prying eyes of jealous spouses, free from all normal restrictions, love in a health farm is Brighton without the guilt, shipboard romance without the wobbles.

Security

In a health farm, security does not refer to the safety of your money or jewels (both locked in the farm's safe for the duration) but to your peace of mind over the two main anxieties of the respective sexes. Men worry over whether to choose a male or female masseur: will the one make a homosexual approach (a groundless fear), will they get an erection when squeezed and rubbed by the other (possibly, but they're much more likely to fall asleep). Women, the observant sex, are worried that a sharp-eyed rival sitting in the steam cabinet will spot when they've been up to no good. 'She's ten minutes late for her massage/why did Mr Johnson come down the other corridor after gym/*both* of them were late for supper again'. Fortunately, in most health farm situations blackmail is possible on both sides.

Warning

Alcohol has twice as potent an effect on the newly cleansed frame. Occasionally, there are frightful goings on in the billiard room after a mass breakout to the pub and the ultimate sanction is applied – people are SENT HOME in disgrace!

Running mates

To the male runner, one of the most agreeable sights in marathon running is the sea of well-shaped female bottoms shimmering ahead of him, and many slowish men, as a matter of policy, select the female with the

SLIM BUT SEXY

'Don't you get tired as you get thinner?' is a question often asked of the amorous male health farm visitor. To which the only answer is 'Do thin men have fewer erections?'

R·U·N·N·I·N·G M·A·T·E·S

Even runners have to take the first step slowly. Good opening lines to jog along with are . . .

- What's your PB?
- Are you entered for the London Mara?
- Where did you get that Nike top?
- I'm in the 5K at Crystal Palace – are you going in for that?
- What a perfectly-developed gluteus maximus!
- If you're turning left, watch for the dog in the third house
- How's your training schedule going?
- Shall we run together tomorrow?

most attractively-shaped rear end on which to fix their sights as they jog along behind.

Like many aspects of running, this pleasing sight is enhanced after a while by the well-known 'runner's high', the pleasurably relaxed state that is felt after 20 or 30 minutes' jogging. So predictable is its onset that during the Jim Fixx era American runners would ask each other 'Have you reached euphoria yet?'

Euphoria is very necessary to runners because many are introverted and self-obsessed, brooding about their Personal Best (PB), and telling you if you give them half a chance how they did 2 hours 44 minutes and 3.4 seconds last time, but the computer prediction says that next time it will only be 2 hours 44 minutes and 3.2 seconds. The specialist computer firms, incidentally, who send back predicted marathon times to hundredths of a second in response to personal data, occupy the same place in the runner's pantheon as astrologers do in the outside world, inspiring the same mixture of hope, superstitious fear, ego trip and guide to compatability between the sexes.

This need for reassurance is not surprising as most serious athletes are terribly worried about their physical functions – their food, their bowels and of course their love lives. Did the kebab they ate last night upset the carefully-planned diet? Will they be able to get to the loo in time before the race? Will they be able to do what that attractive female runner who persuaded them to sign up for a package tour for the New York marathon so obviously expects? Female athletes worry about their centre of gravity, in extreme cases considering bust reduction, and males about how to fight off the dogs that are always attacking joggers. These invariably seem to go for the male

Everyone likes a pleasant view ahead during the long boring hours of the London Marathon.

runner's most sensitive part so that some male joggers are reduced to spraying their shorts with Antimate. And if either sex has forgotten their Vaseline, will Jogger's Nipple cast a blight over their date tonight? But sometimes, romping along through a sunny wood with the birds twittering from leafy bowers in perfect pace with an attractive member of the opposite sex, the dedicated runner finds there are compensations on the lonely and strenuous road to total fitness. On those occasions, Euphoria is reached in a good deal less than 20 minutes.

The pasta party

On the night before the big race, long-distance runners cease to be lonely. All over London, New York, Boston and any other marathon centre there are eve-of-the-race Pasta Parties, where runner Boy meets runner Girl over plates piled with as much spaghetti as they can cram into their stomachs. More formally, this is Part Two of the glycogen bleed-out diet, where you starve your muscles of fuel before a big race so that all the glycogen stores are used up until the night before when, with the muscles desperate for fuel, you give them as much as you can take. To the outside world, this is known as a carbohydrate binge; whatever the title, it is a great way of making new friends.

Mythtake

One of the longest-running myths in recent body history is that of Jogger's Impotence. A few years ago, the serious and respected medical journal *General Practitioner* ran on April 1 a full-page piece which recorded in po-faced terms 'new findings' from a bogus American university supposedly situated in the 'State of Washington'. Non-existent professors were quoted as reporting that the new fitness boom was having a terrible effect on the nation's love life, as male

joggers in vast numbers were becoming impotent. The alleged reason was that their male hormone levels were being seriously impaired by the frequent exercise, and this was attributed to the heat generated by all this exercise, which raised the temperature of the testes, thus diminishing the output of male sex hormones. Few bothered to read to the end of the piece, where the 'head' of the 'Research Department' said that they were now looking at a way of combating this by issuing runners with a small portable refrigerator to be worn in pocket or jock strap; and the story went round the world. 'I still get letters "If I run more than 20 miles a week is there a danger of impotence, and should I take hormone tablets to counteract this"' says Dr David Delvin, Medical Editor of the above journal.

There is, says Dr Delvin, a tiny element of truth in all this. 'An enormous amount of exercise certainly affects female hormones – most women in the top international teams, for instance, have had no periods for quite some time, and gymnasts tend to remain pre-pubertal'.

8 Love in the City

"Lovely lunch hour, darling!"

Like some tiny flower blooming on a galeswept granite cliff, love in the City is a triumph of nature over an inhospitable environment. For the City, of course, is about men making money – for themselves, for other men, for their firms, for the sheer love of it. Indeed, many people say that making money is the City's substitute for making love.

Even the terminology used suggests a strong if suppressed sexual undercurrent. Words like performance and service are in constant use – you are serviced by your broker (where female clients are concerned this is often no more than the literal truth) and you perform for your clients. The market either looks horny or it doesn't, a word that has filtered out from Wall Street through the City's American firms to penetrate even the East End cockney rhyming talk of the bond traders. 'Hey, Kev, what's the market doin'?' 'Got a real salmon and prawn this mornin', Tel.'

Not that sex is frowned on *per se*. It is simply seen as an unnecessary distraction from the real business in hand: the day-long, day-in, day-out concentration on building an ever bigger and better bank account. Nevertheless, even for the most self-centred, the opportunities are there ...

City types

Though the single, unifying common denominator in the City is the never-ending urge to make money, secondary sexual characteristics vary considerably from one City type to another.

The merchant banker

The most rarified and gentlemanly attitudes are found in the merchant banks,

Late-home-again excuses

- Sorry, darling, we're getting wiped out here – you know we've got three million sterling? Well, it's dropping like a stone and we've got to unwind it pretty damn quick.
- Sorry, darling, my best client's just called and he wants to see me NOW.
- Sorry, darling, my second-best client's just called and he wants to see me NOW.
- Don't be like that, sweetheart, you know this man is 25 per cent of my business – *our* business – so I've GOT to go.
- Listen, darling, I'm taking some of my clients racing and I won't be back for dinner.
- I've got to have a drink with a client after work.
- I've got to have a drink with an analyst after work.
- I've got to have a drink with a broker after work.
- I've got to have a drink with a bond trader after work.
- I've *got* to have a drink.

where the atmosphere is that of a first-class library and most of the staff have a good Oxbridge degree (if the bank is feeling exceptionally adventurous, it may occasionally admit someone from Exeter, Durham, or even Bristol). The result is that something of the undergraduate swot still lingers on; many young bankers, getting to the office long before the official start to the day and working late, have little energy for an active social life every night – though stockbrokers claim that even bankers and insurance people get worked up at the Christmas party.

All bankers are conscious of the image the Bank wants them to present, so wear its uniform of dark suit, discreet shirt and tie – though nobody wears old school ties any more since wearing the O.E. tie became unpopular with Etonians. Young bankers know their girl friends are seriously attracted when they give them a Hermes tie (which is also what stockbrokers give young bankers when they want to show that they too are serious). When bankers lunch people it is called 'marketing', and is noted down in Economist diaries.

As merchant banking is regarded as more intellectually respectable than the more market-oriented jobs, nobody minds admitting to it at a cocktail party (occasionally sensitive stockbrokers have been known to leave this lucrative profession after sear-

ing experiences at North London dinner parties). Here, although Morgan Grenfell, Rothschilds and Hambros are the blue chip banks, Warburg people gain an unfair advantage with girls with their fascinating opening gambit: 'I wasn't allowed on the strength until my handwriting had been analysed'.

Opportunities in the City

• • •

often have to be seized at a moment's notice:

- I've got to go to a meeting and I won't be back until after lunch.
- It's a bit slack at the moment, so I'm going to take an hour off to play squash.
- I'm doing a Road Show, so I'll see you tomorrow.
- I'm meeting a client, so I'll see you later on.

For anyone in corporate finance, the best all-round, all-purpose and uncheckable excuse for an all-night absence is 'I'm going to the printers'. Proof-checking on a new issue, which can go on until 3.00 am, is vital – unless you want to lose the company millions.

Fund managers

Fund managers (apart from those in banks, who are bound by the Bank's code) don't dress nearly so smartly – many are quite shabby. But then, fund managers don't have to make an effort; constantly fêted by brokers and salesmen, their chief task is to keep their heads level enough to make the right decisions over the vast quantities of money they have in their power to invest. Fund management used to be a backwater but now recruits professionally; it is popular with women, which makes the endless lunching more enjoyable for brokers.

Etonian or Ex-Brigade seldom went to university. They enjoy killing things, especially things that fly, so are seldom seen in August when they disappear to shoot or cruise round the Grecian islands – when they will invariably ring in to the office ostensibly to see what's going on but really because the yacht has a radio telephone which they enjoy playing with and showing off. (American brokers, who are paranoid about competition, only take holidays when ordered to do so on pain of instant collapse by their doctors.)

Brokers are the most sexually arrogant

> ❦❦ *Brokers are the most sexually arrogant men in the City and most are convinced they are irresistible to women* ❧❧

Bankers, fund managers and people in the major insurance firms see romance in terms of being settled and stable: a foundation to life to be achieved as quickly as possible so that they don't have to spend a lot of time thinking about Love – time which could be devoted to the real business of life, making money. The result is that they are excellent marriage prospects for the determined and homeloving girl, as most ask for no more than peace and domesticity on their arrival back from the office.

Go for broker

People on the Sell side of the Street* are quite a different glass of champagne. Stockbrokers drive Porsches and Ferraris instead of the Golfs and BMWs of insurance and investment, and though frequently Old

men in the City and most are convinced they are irresistible to women. So not surprisingly, the brokerage industry is renowned for passion. Younger brokers go to cocktail parties every evening because if they've not married they are permanently out on the scout, older ones belong to clubs like Boodles or Whites where they drop in for a drink when they've missed the 6.30 to Basingstoke; all of them belong to Annabel's where they spend a lot of time drinking champagne. They also spend a lot of time drinking champagne in other places and if this habit is mentioned, smile engagingly and say 'It's a bull market'.

*One of the few printable American expressions that have infiltrated the City. 'Street' here refers to Wall Street.

C·A·R·R·Y·I·N·G ON

It's Longchamps and the sun is shining, but a good City man always studies the odds before making his move.

When a broker has launched a successful affair with a money manager (one of the commonest combinations), he can frequently spend all day with his inamorata by dint of the lavish entertaining which is part and parcel of the brokerage industry's life. A box at Ascot, the Derby or Wimbledon, a day at the races or polo (all, almost needless to say, floated on a sea of champagne), possibly a flight to Le Mans, Monte Carlo or Paris for the Arc, to which the loved one is asked along with other guests provides the perfect cover – or, in stockbroking parlance, 'I was able to bury it'.

As brokers never have to say 'I'm afraid you've got to work too, darling, and we mustn't have children just yet because we can't afford it', they are not particularly interested in a woman's brains or career potential. The only thing a broker does insist on in a female companion is that she's stylish and presentable; because he earns so much he always goes to the best restaurants and he certainly doesn't want to be seen out with some dog (as his friends will inevitably describe her the next morning). Though brokers and feminist women are not natural bedmates, the broker – always generously tolerant towards the female sex – is prepared to make an exception, provided, as one of them put it, 'she screws, and she screws well'.

The American sub-species

Even in the highly-charged atmosphere of the brokerage industry, one sub-species stands out. As all who have come into even the most peripheral contact with them agree, the American broking fraternity are the most tireless bunch of sexual athletes in the entire western world. Here are some sample tributes.

'Quite simply, the randiest bunch of men I've ever met.' 'I've now worked in six American firms and I can state with complete confidence that the American stockbroker is the horniest male I've ever come across.' 'No woman is safe anywhere near these men. I wish I could say the same of our boys.'

Neither established liaisons nor age act as a brake: stories of the legendary feats of the most senior partners are recounted in awed tones. 'There was this old guy, semi-retired, but every day at 12.00 sharp he nipped out for the same arrangement he'd had for the past 25 years – different girls, of course. Said he couldn't function without a Nooner.' AND they make more money than anyone else in the Square Mile.

The analyst

Another example of American influence in the City is the increasing number of Analysts (researchers who can forecast share performance). 'In the old days, you were able to say "I think you ought to have a few of these" and the client would buy' says one stockbroker, 'now, you actually have to give them decent reasons.' Analysis is one of the City jobs that attracts women; and the pretty young analyst is a natural focus for the stockbroker's attention, especially as stockbrokers and analysts often go round in pairs when making a particularly forceful or competitive play for new business. Senior

The Lady Analyst's Tale

'You're sitting across a lunch table with a client and you're telling him why he should put his billion into this company or that, but after you've settled all that you have to talk about something else, so you start on what kind of cars you both have and where you park them. As you sat down he'll have glanced ever so casually at your hand to see if you're wearing a wedding ring, and if you're not the next thing he'll say is, "What did you do for your holiday this year?" So you tell him, and he tells you about his. And then he'll say, ever so casually "Oh, did you go alone?" If you say, "No, I went with my boy friend" there's an immediate change of attitude; if you say, "Yes", you just have to wait for the inevitable invitatation. About 50 per cent of single men get round in one way or another to asking you out.'

partners who want to teach brash young juniors a lesson send them out with male analysts with spectacles and dandruff.

Dealers

Even within the soberer confines of the investment management business there is a certain group of portfolio and fund managers known to each other as 'Dealers'. To be described by one of this dashing band as a Real Dealer means you have achieved the coveted reputation of being, as one of them puts it, 'as horny as any broker'.

The female stockbroker

Female stockbrokers, a gradually increasing band, are invariably young and attractive, and the buzz goes round very fast if there's a new one in town. Male fund managers who have previously given up an hour of their precious time to the female stockbroker's male predecessor only after months of besieging, frequently do the unthinkable and make the first call themselves. 'We used to talk to Jeremy but as he's not covering the account any more we thought we'd introduce ourselves. Perhaps we could meet for lunch to discuss things in more detail?'

Many portfolio managers carry this attitude to extremes, considering that as it is the female broker's job to take them out to dinner and entertain them, they might as well jump on her bones afterwards (see

'Dealers'). Female brokers who find this prospect pleasing always say: 'You do realise I'm not just doing this because I'm in the brokerage business and you're a portfolio manager?'

Making the most of it

Although the City is a hive of gossip and rumour and all the offices are jam-packed, even this can be turned to advantage. Since everyone can always hear what everyone else is saying, the phrase, 'Let's have a drink after work' simply means there is some idea you don't want the rest of the world to know about. Because of the crowding, and the stress, tempers fray – sometimes brokers crack and throw television screens across the room, but more often they shout at a secretary. Naturally, this makes a good excuse for the nearest man to reach out with a comforting arm – if she sheds a tear, there is a general rush.

He travels the most enjoyably who travels alone

People in the City travel surprisingly frequently. Bankers zoom off to Paris to assess the performance of French companies and, if they can fix this for a Friday or a Monday, with luck they can spend the weekend assessing the performance of a different kind of company. Fund managers can disappear to Japan for a fortnight; brokers can jet to New York at any time provided they can think of a plausible excuse; and bond dealers have an annual saturnalia at some lucky European city, where they all get blind drunk and are liable to be caught by the police driving unsteadily down the road in a vain search for the red light district.

Those who wish to deter their wives from accompanying them on such trips arrange for accommodation at the nastiest

The rule about not getting involved with a colleague is never more important than when on a business trip with an attractive member of the opposite sex. Tempting though it may be to make the fullest possible use of the romantic delights of the Mandarin hotel, thanks to today's improved communications, every detail of the previous night's rendezvous is flashed back to the office on the telex along with the price of Sony or Hitachi – or worse still, appears on one of the director's VDU terminals.

tence correctly, can shout the odds like any trackside bookie. They wear expensive Italian shoes with gold chains, have custom-built Rollers with their initials as number plates, send each other gorillagrams for their birthday and are all under 30 (while still able to do the job at 27, you are too old

In the City, even saying 'Happy Birthday' is a deeply businesslike event.

hotel in the town instead of their usual room at the Splendide, travel on to the next destination on a stopping train that necessitates rising at 4.00 am, and wind up with dinner with their grossest and most primitive client, arranging for their loved one to sit opposite him as he blows cigar smoke into her face, leers at the floor show and, with luck, picks his nose. After such an experience few wives, however persuasively pressed, will consent to accompany their husbands a second time.

The money men

The quickest way of earning a lot of money in the City is through bond trading or Foreign Exchange dealing (i.e., buying dollars and selling pounds on a very large scale indeed).

Classically, Foreign Exchange dealers are from the East End (the only dealing room which employs graduates is Citibank, who regard themselves as the best), started as barrow boys or taxi drivers and, though often unable to articulate a complete sento be recruited). At Foreign Exchange lunches the big decision is whether to order the most expensive bottle of wine on the menu or stay with the shorts (double Bacardi and coke is the favourite); statistically, money broking is well above the average for alcoholism, even though the days of helping yourself to vodka at 10.00 am from the dealing-room fridge have more or less gone.

Money broking offices are devoid of love in every sense – no chat about dinner with the beautiful girl last night, not even the more or less obligatory dirty jokes, just West Ham and money, money, money. If business is coolish, money brokers rush out for an hour's squash; nevertheless, the hours are so long (from 7.00 am until drinks with the client after work finishes), the stress so enormous and the split in lifestyles between him and her so dramatic that money broking has a notoriously high divorce rate.

As local heroes earning more than anyone else, they married the best girl in the street when they started but by the time they've moved up to international top hotels and first class travel round the world, she's begun to complain they're never at home. And though they go on enormously expensive holidays, taking the whole family to Disneyland or Barbados, they stay in the same small house in Chigwell because they haven't time to look for a nicer one elsewhere. Their shoes are clean because there's a shoeshine machine on the landing to smarten them up when they go off to see bankers but their suits are off the peg because they're far too frantic to go to a tailor; and they *certainly* haven't time to look for a new type of girl. So when the divorce is through, they probably marry their best friend's ex-wife.

Sometimes women try their hand at money broking but few can stand the screaming, shouting, and naked competitiveness coupled with the stress of finding a million pounds in a few minutes which a normal day's work consists of. But as the bond room view of woman's role in society is, to say the least, primitive, this is probably a blessing in disguise.

'The biggest change in the City is that women have come in and the obligatory brandy at the end of lunch has gone.'

<small>SENIOR PARTNER, INSURANCE FIRM</small>

❦❦*When the divorce is through, they probably marry their best friend's ex-wife* ❦❦

The native women

Women in the City fall into two categories: executives (i.e., those doing the same jobs as men), and the larger class comprising secretaries, telephone and telex operators. Almost all the second group come from areas handy for London Bridge or Liverpool Street stations, which in practice means Kent, Essex, north and especially east London.

Telex operators

These are short busty girls called Cheryl or Lynn who are almost always from the East End – at one time every outgoing or incom-

Cooking directors' lunches is jolly good practice for all those dinner parties later on when you've eventually got a director all of your own.

ing telex message of any importance was signed off with the words 'George Davis is innocent'. Telex girls can all take care of themselves.

Secretaries

These vary from the more voluptuous blowsily attractive girls found in the rougher all-male industries like bond dealing or Foreign Exchange to neat efficient girls called Sue from Hertfordshire suburbs who are lightning with word processors. The loucher sort of City man considers young and pretty City secretaries, safely out of touch with anything to do with his own home life,

background or postal district, to be his natural preserve rather in the way some doctors think they have a *droit de practitioner* with the nurses.

Despite its potential as husband-hunting territory and the high rates of pay (roughly double those of the West End) no Sloane will take a City secretarial job – too far from Harrods, can't meet friends for shopping or lunch and not what Sloanes call 'interesting'. Besides, there's a row if you're late for work two days running, expect to leave for the weekend after lunch on Friday, or use the word processor to answer wedding invitations. Sloanes do cook the directors' lunches, though, often discussing this at the next night's cocktail party ('Do you do your marketing at Smithfield, Caroline, or just go to Cobb's?') where they are quite likely to meet some of the young bankers and brokers they have just been cooking for.

Executive women

These are a different breed altogether, and immediately distinguishable from secretaries by their clothes – a played-down form of power dressing which involves silk shirts, expensive shoes, a skirt version of the business suit (executive women never wear trousers) and crocodile briefcases. Most are under 30: 1977 was the year that saw the real lowering of the drawbridge, with today's Oxbridge milk round now trawling as much female talent as male.

But keeping up with the Samuels and Montagues mean long hours, unflinching concentration and a hard-edged competitiveness that pushes the idea of childbearing and, in consequence, often marriage to one side. So for the young woman executive, love in the City is usually with an older or

---

> ## HOW TO APPROACH
> ## THE NEWEST YOUNG WOMAN EXECUTIVE
>
> - I've got an idea I want to talk to you about but I don't want to make too much noise about it in the office.
>   Shall we say Coates' in half an hour?
>
> ## HOW NOT TO APPROACH
> ## THE LATEST-JOINED YOUNG
> ## WOMAN EXECUTIVE
>
> - Oh, it is nice to see a pretty young female face here!

---

more senior man, often in an extension of the Mentor principle – if only because the boys she joined with are her most immediate and fiercest rivals.

'It gets to the stage where the people working with you won't even take a message when you've gone to the john,' says one girl. '"Can't see her anywhere, she must have gone" they say and put the phone down. They'll do anything to impede your progress.' And while men only a few years older feel threatened by a bright young female just a step or two below them, a senior of 45 is merely flattered by her attention. On the practical side, he is one of the few people there to have an office to himself so the occasional indiscreet telephone call is possible – although even the non-compromising

NOW MISS TATTERSHALL, DON'T YOU TAKE ANY GYP FROM THE RANDY YOUNG BUCKS DOWN STAIRS WHO'LL BE FAWNING ALL OVER YOU

monosyllables at her end can be a giveaway. It's not so much that the close proximity in the average City office allows every word to be heard as the fact that all training is based on the need to have one ear cocked for what's happening elsewhere as well as to what you yourself are doing.

Girls who do carry on with senior men in their own or other offices try desperately hard to keep it secret. Not for any reasons of morality or fear of being involved in a divorce – senior partners commute from Hampshire or Sussex and anyway wives seldom penetrate the City – but because it will damage their professional image. 'So that's how she pulled off that deal' colleagues will mutter disparagingly.

Nevertheless, the giveaway signs are there for those who know how to look for them (and everyone does). However carefully they leave from separate exits, someone will spot them in the same wine bar half an hour later; however often he leaves the building ten minutes ahead of her, someone is bound to pass him waiting for no appar-

> ❦❦ *If I reject the client who has tried to pounce on me, will he be so cross he takes his business elsewhere?* 🐦🐦

ent purpose on a street corner. And if they set forth openly together to play an innocent game of squash – well, what a coincidence to run across them sharing an early dinner together not too far from the station two hours later. Sometimes, desperation lends ingenuity (and especially since that last resort of the desperate, the 14 secluded arches of the old car park at Liverpool Street Station, has now been pulled down). One girl and her lover would meet in the lift, entering it at basement and ground floor

respectively at an hour when few people were around, and jamming on the Stop button between floors.

City girls contemplating an affair outside the office can also find themselves faced with dilemmas to do with work. Roughly

> ❦❦ *If I welcome his advances, will he think it's only because I want his business?* 🐦🐦

summed up, it runs something like this: If I reject the client who has tried to pounce on me, will he be so cross he takes his business elsewhere? Alternatively if I welcome his advances will he think it's only because I want his business? And explaining the real reason for the sudden withdrawal of a valuable portfolio will only confirm some of the older members' more chauvinist prejudice.

For the truth is that while affairs in no way reflect on a City man's professional image or integrity, it is quite the reverse with a woman. Nobody would dream of holding such a natural and feminine activity as falling in love against that charming and efficient Ms Smith, but bang goes her credibility in the market place. Though nobody, of course, would dream of using the words *Double Standard*.

There's no such thing as a free lunch

The City's *l'heure bleue* is the lunch hour, when Romance frequently makes its heady appearance either under cover of a business deal or, more likely, to disguise the fact that one is in the offing. As the people who manage the big pools of money are

T·H·E A·P·A·R·T·M·E·N·T

One major obstacle to the consummation of love in the City is the shameful lack of both hotels and apartment houses. Although one enterprising senior stockbroker has an application to open a brothel lodged with the City of London authorities ready for the moment when the Government finally yields to popular demand and licences them, the general consensus is that if the Barbican did not exist, it would have been necessary to invent it. In most offices, someone has a flat in one of these fortress-like towers, and the key is thrown around either on a rota system (c.f. that excellently observed movie *The Apartment*), or acquired by whatever method of blackmail is to hand. Only those in Lloyds take out a premium against the lock sticking when it's their turn.

endlessly chased, it is vital to find some way to jump the queue. And often, the easiest method of approach to an elusive portfolio or fund manager is to get on good terms with his/her secretary, who will fix up an appointment for you, put you through when you telephone, or signal to her boss to hang up on one of your rivals if your call is waiting.

The simplest way of ensuring the friendliness and co-operation of these invaluable girls is, in the words of one half-million a year broker, 'to take her out to lunch and fill her up with champagne'. Naturally, one thing often leads to another.

Once the relationship has been formed and the client hooked, further time must be set aside for maintaining it – a woman spurned means business landing in the lap of your rivals, so successful brokers lunch regularly with a whole harem of girls.

If the client, too, turns out to be female

and attractive, lunch offers the perfect cover for the unobtrusive launch of a romance – the money manager who isn't taken out to lunch does not exist. It only remains to add that when hands meet over unfolded prospectuses, slipping between the balance sheets together often follows.

Where to drink your lunch

The best-known champagne bar is The Greenhouse (always known as Green's), daily filled to the brim with jobbers and bond dealers, though in the Christmas run-up famous wine bars like Coates or the Bow Wine Vaults serve little else but champagne – in fact the whole Square Mile nearly sinks beneath a tidal wave of Veuve Cliquot, Bollinger and Krug. Money brokers take their clients to expensive restaurants like Le Poulbot in Cheapside or Corney and Barrow where you can pay £55 for the wine alone; companies make presentations at the Savoy; brokers take clients to Tante Claire, Boulestin's or the Interlude de Tabaillau. For those who find the idea of lunch without some kind of sexual *frisson* intolerable, there is the Paris Grill – girls with sprayed-on jeans and sexy French accents, a notable beauty at the Marmiton and, for the more voyeuristic, the City Circle, with its emphasis on costumes made from fishnet.

❝ When hands meet over unfolded prospectuses, slipping between the balance sheets together often follows ❞

9 Love in Westminster

Views on the amount of love going on at any one time in Westminster vary widely. Some say there is less adultery (though not fornication) than for any other group of people of similar age, social standing and financial status; others maintain with equal positiveness that MPs are always at it. Since most Honourable Members quite relish the idea of being thought of as saucy rogues in general terms, they do nothing to discourage this impression – except, of course, when it begins to have a personal bite.

Looking for an audience

The truth lies somewhere in between. Womanising is a hobby which like any other demands time, effort, money and thought. Although people who are good at politics tend to have a lot of energy – and surplus energy usually means sex – the typical MP's deepest and most frenzied desire is for an audience rather than a lover. If you are the kind of man (because the number of women MPs is still so shamefully small Honourable Members are referred to as 'he' throughout this chapter for the sake of convenience) whose idea of a good night out is to stand in a dusty hall haranguing those half dozen members of the East Wittering Labour Party who have been good enough to walk through the pouring rain to hear you, then you are probably not the sort of chap whose spare moments are spent arranging secret assignations with beautiful women. On the other hand, those MPs who do see themselves as great lovers make more of a song and dance about it than people in other walks of life, thanks both to the feeling that anything they do is important and therefore worth making known, and the complementary conviction that *anything* is better than not being noticed.

One fact is indisputable. Apart from London members who perforce return to their own hearths every night, the MP not only has a cast-iron reason for being away from home from Monday to Thursday for 32 out of the 52 weeks, plus a pied-à-terre paid for by the taxpayer (and what other profession can boast a subsidised love nest?), but his domestic affairs are largely unknown to the rest of his 649 confrères. The average Conservative MP knows the wives of only about a dozen of his friends, the Labour member fewer still, so if a woman of uncertain provenance is seen on the arm of the Honourable Member for Middleford West both friend and foe will give him the benefit of the doubt. Nor – as in the school which the House of Commons resembles in so many way – would one MP ever dream of shopping another. Especially to his wife.

As a lover, the MP has his idiosyncrasies,

AND · WHERE · WERE · *YOU*

LAST

NIGHT?

'At 10.00 pm I was voting,' says the MP virtuously. 'Then we had the third reading of the Social Security Bill – Norman made an *extremely* good speech.'

Few wives would have an answer to that one; and only the mistress familiar with House of Commons procedure would even dream of suspecting that the MP's actual whereabouts were not unadjacent to the well-appointed Pimlico flat of the well-appointed lady television researcher on whose programme he is appearing next week.

'You can always blind nice women with science,' says one veteran backbench Lothario. 'Clever or suspicious ones look at the whip every week.'

This vital document is delivered to the MP every Friday and contains the Parliamentary programme for the coming week; depending on its importance to the Government, each subject is underlined twice, three times (hence the expression Three-Line Whip) or not at all. Anyone who can crack its fairly complicated code will be able to give the unfaithful MP a nasty jolt ('But, darling, there *wasn't* a vote on Tuesday night! So where did you say you were?')

Nevertheless, it has to be stated that the favourite all-purpose, all-Party excuse still remains unbreakable. For economy, ease and effectiveness, there is nothing to touch: 'Something's cropped up at the House'.

chief of which are vanity, egocentricity, and a passion amounting almost to idolatry for the sound of his own voice. Along with the user-friendly handshakes, camera-ready smiles and ability to spot their own name in smudged type in the stop press over someone else's shoulder, goes a terrifying articulacy. Rare indeed is the Honourable Member who cannot talk for 20 minutes on, for or against any subject, irrespective of whether he knows anything about it, at the drop of a despatch box.

'Don't you think you've had enough?'

Naturally enough, the chief requirement of wife or girl friend is being a good listener, with a sense of humour defined as *Laughing at My Jokes*. As listening to the MP speak in the typical Parliamentary debate is one of the most searching tests of true love known to man, one of the quickest ways of spotting Westminster romances is to look round the gallery during an important debate. The coy glances shot up towards the assortment of pretty women gazing down with rapt attention and admiration are not a sign that the MP has scored a major point in the heated argument about nuclear power waste but a confession of hopeless passion.

The cardinal sin for wife or girl friend is to interrupt the MP when he is in full flow. She must also keep a keen eye on his drink consumption while not appearing in any way to monitor it. The MP's inner image of himself is as a sophisticated, witty, idealistic and forceful lawmaker, selfless in his pursuit of the public weal and irresistible to women; saying 'Don't you think you've had enough?'

does not blend easily with this picture. But as drink only enhances the MP's natural sense of his own importance and urge towards aggressiveness (all MPs love a good row) – the truly devoted wife has to develop a sixth sense as to the location of the drinks table in any gathering.

She must also take care not to be a source of trouble herself; i.e., just enough leg showing to do him credit but not a neckline low enough to start people talking. She should also be prepared to talk to all the boring people her husband avoids like the plague on whatever pretext floats into his head at that moment, but whose continued support is essential to the Party – let alone her better half.

MPs old-style

'I represent' are probably the two commonest words in the MP's vocabulary. When he is not claiming to stand for democracy, the White Fish Trade, the rights of the underdog or All Decent Men and Women in This Country, what he represents most frequently are My Constituents.

But does he? While the Member may share proclivities and personality traits with those he represents, occupationally

AND WHAT WAS THE RIGHT HONOURABLE'S MEMBER UP TO LAST NIGHT?

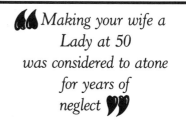

❛❛ Making your wife a Lady at 50 was considered to atone for years of neglect ❜❜

the House of Commons is far from being a cross-section of the country. One in six MPs is a lawyer of some kind; journalists, homosexuals and media people generally appear in higher-than-average proportions on both sides as do (on the Labour side) teachers.

Old-style Tory MPs had polished complexions, an expensive education, and hair that looked as if it had been brushed backward from birth with a pair of ivory-handled hairbrushes. Many of them discreetly married each others' wives, the advantage to this arrangement being that they took on someone already familiar with the duties of a Tory MP's consort (if shy, the old-style Tory MP would marry his secretary, often the first woman since Nanny with whom he had had a real relationship); and after years of unquestioning support of the Party through thick, thin, and the most morally dubious of political manoeuvres, were given knighthoods – making your wife a Lady at 50 was considered to atone for years of neglect.

MPs new-style

New-style Tory MPs wear ready-made suits, springier hair, bank at Lloyds rather than Coutts, jog to work at Westminster from their Clapham bedsits, and are much less discreet in their love affairs. When one MP, scourge of the Café Royal, left his wife, he called a press conference with the woman he had left his wife for, sitting by his side.

Labour MPs are shorter, fatter, frequently bearded and go angling where Tories fish. They split fairly neatly into the old Trade Union MP and the newer group, go-getting young poly lecturers who are basically middle class but pretending to be workers (new style Tory MPs, incidentally, invariably claim engineer, miner or bus-driver grandfathers). Many of the ones most famous for noise are quiet as lambs at home.

Affairs don't often happen between Honourable Members because there is such a shortage of lady MPs, with comparatively few of those affair material. Nevertheless, there are quite often cases of intense but unrequited admiration. These 'crushes', which still further increase the resemblance of the Mother of Parliaments to a vast, unruly school, quickly become well known and the subject of general hilarity, not to say ribaldry.

Both sides tend to regard Tory women at Westminster as more attractive than Labour ones: Tory MPs out of a sense of loyalty (the one essential quality for all Conservatives), Labour MPs because the twinsets, pearls and bouffant hairdos of the Tory women opposite them add an exotic social dimension missing from the home team, thus allowing them to fantasise in some detail about interestingly earthy relationships with the distant and rather aristocratic creatures opposite, during longueurs in debates on the datestamping of petfood or compulsory fluoridation.

The secretary keeping the Member under control

House of Commons secretaries are a special breed, combining efficiency, political acumen and organisational power with sexual clout. They work in offices all round Westminster serving (if that is the word) at least three Members of Parliament each and forming among themselves a lightning, invisi-

'The haroosh that follows the intermittent revelation of the sexual goings-on of an unlucky MP has convinced me that the only safe pleasure for a Parliamentarian is a bag of boiled sweets.'

JULIAN CRITCHLEY, MP,

in *Westminster Blues*

ble, all-pervasive communications network that makes British Telecom seem something out of the steam age.

Some have joined this dedicated band with one simple aim in view: to become an MP's wife. Others are passionate about politics, frequently with the ambition of becoming an MP themselves, and for these girls, going to bed with an Honourable Member is simply an osmotic extension of the career process, making it into the body politic by making a body political, you might say. Irrespective of party, the Whips' Office is famous for pretty and amusing secretaries; here conviviality is the watchword, whisky starts circulating at six in the evening, and there is a constant flow of people in and out, none of whom seems to have a wife living in London.

Secretaries who work in Old Palace Yard (otherwise known as the Gin Palace) are often single or between husbands. Here is the heartland of those secretaries who have had ongoing affairs with their Members of such long duration that the happy pair have reached the patience-playing stage and everyone takes the whole thing for granted. For although the Member is never going to leave his wife, both sides are caught like flies in honey by the fact that his work is the consuming interest of both of them.

Secretaries fall into two main categories: those who have their Member well under control, opening and answering all his letters without benefit of his advice, managing the day to their own satisfaction and reappearing at 6.00 with a sheaf of neatly-typed,

Many MPs marry their secretaries ...

and many don't ...

HAVE
YOU MET
JILL ...?

Such are the demands on an MP's time and
knowledge that alibis for being in the presence of a
lovely young woman are almost infinite.
Try these for size ...

—————— · ——————

★ Jill is helping me with my research.

—————— · ——————

★ I'm picking Jill's brains on social work – she helps deprived children
in East Hackney.

—————— · ——————

★ Jill's helping me out with the paperwork on this Bill.

—————— · ——————

★ My secretary's on holiday and Jill's kindly giving me a hand.

—————— · ——————

★ Jill's the daughter of an old family friend/valued constituent and I'm
showing her round the House.

well-phrased and sensible communications
for him to sign; and those who feel their
Member should be consulted about what
will be going out in his name. This lot offer
a better prospect for Members on the prowl.

For with a little judicious weighing-up of
the merits of this approach or that, a lively
anecdote or two, 'Going Through the Post'
can be spun out until the morning committees rise, when the magic phrase 'Why don't
we continue this on the Terrace?' (see
below) or 'Shall we talk about this one over a
drink?' can be brought into play.

Later on, 'Listen, I've got to go into
Questions – why don't we finish this off at
5.00?' can be used as an alternative. Later
still, dinner ('Oh God – I've made you too
late for the shops again') can be suggested.

Wary secretaries realise here what sort of
man they are in for. Mean members say
'Join me for bacon and eggs in the canteen',
scattering papers around the table to show
the essential innocence of the whole thing;
those clearly signalling their intentions,

order a second bottle of wine with brandy to
follow, when the offer of a lift home will,
with luck, be accepted.

For what could be more economically
and sexually satisfying for the poor but
personable Member looking for a base in
London than the attractive and indepen-
dant secretary with her own car, a passionate interest in the furthering of his career,
and a flat conveniently near Westminster?

It only remains to add that the truly
devoted secretary provides an answer to the
school of thought that believes all MPs
should be provided with dogs by the taxpayer because only dogs give the uncritical
admiration and unswerving loyalty so
essential to the MP's inner wellbeing. The
right secretary will do something of the
same, proof being the large number of
Honourable Members who have snapped
up one of these paragons in marriage.

The researcher

Many MPs now employ researchers as well
as or instead of secretaries. This is because
their services come cheap – even, sometimes, with a cash bonus for the MP. For the
corridors of the Palace of Westminster are
becoming ever fuller of college students
from abroad, placed there by specialist companies to continue their political studies *and
actually paying the MP for the privilege!*

No wonder the Researcher of the right
type (young, beautiful, foreign and anxious
to get to grips with her subject) is the kind of

*❦❦ All MPs should be provided
with dogs by the taxpayer
because only dogs give
the uncritical admiration
and unswerving loyalty
so essential to the MP's
inner wellbeing ❦❦*

HANDY EXCUSES

The MP has innumerable handy excuses with which to bamboozle just about
everyone – his wife, his mistress, his friends, his constituents, or somebody whose
dinner party he wishes to drop out of. Here is a typical scene . . .

Morning.

The MP (virtuously): 'There's no Three-liner today, darling.
I'll be home to supper.'

Evening

(His pretty, young research assistant has just admitted that Yes, she could be free
for dinner): 'Oh, hello darling – look, I'm terribly sorry, the Secretary of State
wants to see me and the only time he can fit me in is 9.00. No, I don't know
what's involved or whether I'll have to do anything about it there and then. So
expect me when you see me . . .'

---

affair-material fantasies are woven of. Will
she be a keen, young American from Ohio
State with drum-majorette legs and a campus queen smile? Or an Australian who,
with luck, will have her fair share of that
refreshing Antipodean characteristic, a total
lack of inhibition? Yes, she is the Right Stuff
with a vengeance, even down to the fact that
the affair has a built-in time limit: she is only
able to spend daddy's money looking after
you at the House of Commons for three or
four months because next term she has to
go back and write her thesis. So after a
touching and string-free farewell, both of
you can go on your way with beautiful
memories and a stack of notes – hers to be
typed up later, and yours in the bank.

There is only one detectable flaw in The
Researcher as a species. Quite a number are
male.

The whip

The first requirement for every whip – and
especially the Chief Whip – is a dirty mind.
A Whip should *always* think the worst. In
more than one famous case of politico-
sexual scandal the parties concerned have
made little or no attempt at concealment,
perhaps on the theory that nothing deceives
like complete openness. But a Chief Whip
with the proverb 'There is no smoke without the possibility of a raging inferno that
could consume us all' engraved on his mind
would see through even the most sophisticated double bluff and fix them both.

The ideal nose for what might bring a
Government into disrepute was displayed
by an earlier Chief Whip. When one new
building was opened as offices for MPs,
many Honourable Members wanted locks
on the doors; but realising the only reason
they wanted this total security was for
Ugandan-style research, the Chief Whip
refused, on the grounds that if the building

EXPECT ME
WHEN YOU SEE ME

'Oh hello – is that you, darling? Look, Charles is away and they asked
me to fill in. I felt I had to say Yes – and of course it means I'll be able
to get a night off Charles later. So expect me when you see me . . .'

caught fire he would have to go round every room unlocking people too preoccupied to notice any whiff of burning or alternatively making sure there was no one there. 'I'm not going to risk incineration simply so that fellow Members can get up to a bit of nookie' was the phrase used by this perceptive and sensible man. The only person eventually allowed a lock on the door was a certain Scots MP, member of an all-Party Committee on Scotch whisky and representative of a constituency that included distillers, who expressed the well-founded fear that fellow Members might come into his room to steal the whisky kept in it for testing

purposes. Few other stories express the twin priorities of Honourable Members so succinctly.

Tempting tipples – choosing the right bar

No picture of love in Westminster would be complete without a reference to the consumption of alcohol. For the river of drink that flows down MPs' throats is comparable in size and volume to the one outside. Each party has its preference. Labour MPs drink the standard Party tipple, Federation Ale, a peculiarly potent brew with a heavily diure-

PARTY LINES

In Westminster, even love splits down party lines.

TORY
Tory Party Associations take much more of an interest in the Member's private life although, where once they used to look askance at all divorce whether or not the Member was the guilty party, now they only mind if there is a lot of bloodshed and acrimony. For what they don't welcome is massive scandal: it is being found out, rather than the actual misbehaviour, that does for Cabinet Ministers.

Tory wives are almost as much in the front line as their husbands, especially when it comes to Selection Committees. Conservative MP Julian Critchley quotes the occasion when he was adopted for Aldershot in 1970 from a short list of three. 'A nice old colonel living in Fleet came up to me and said, "I bet you don't know why we chose you? It was your wife – a damn fine woman!" It transpired that at the

end of the selection interviews each of the three wives in turn was asked the same questions, and Heather was the only one who got to her feet – there's Cheltenham Ladies' College for you.' Such a scene is unimaginable in the Labour Party.

Once married, the Tory wife plays a much greater rôle in the constituency than her Labour counterpart, sometimes even doing her husband's surgery for him at weekends and making speeches, opening bazaars or presenting prizes as a matter of course.

LABOUR
In the Labour Party, wives tend either actually to run it (Glenys Kinnock) or have nothing to do with it (the vast majority). So those Labour members who marry, re-marry, and re-re-marry have no problems with either the constituency or their colleagues: they don't take their wives to the former and simply introduce the current spouse as My Wife to the latter.

But although Labour have never bothered much about how their members occupy their spare time, and the Labour MP is much freer to come and go (or as one Honourable Member thoughtfully put it, to go and come), within the Party itself love has become more difficult, thanks largely to the forceful and pervasive presence of the new equality. 'Twenty years ago it was possible to pat a lady's bottom without being arrested,' says one Labour MP nostalgically. 'Now, the mildest double entendre is likely to lead at best to a slapped face or a charge of sexual harassment, at worst to a critical resolution before the General Management Committee.'

Where Tory women meet to plan the social function in constituency or area – or even to prepare the coffee for the men discussing politics next door – Labour women have badges saying *Labour Women Make Policy Not Tea*. Labour Party female activists are much more involved politically and much

tic effect; Tory MPs prefer whisky or gin. Only when being ahead in the opinion polls allows them to shift from a pose of lofty moral superiority do S.D.P. MPs indulge in a hefty slug of whisky though claret is typically their favourite drink. For those Members forced by prudence on the pleas of their medical advisers onto the wagon, the most popular drink is a Strawberry Blonde (tonic and bitters).

There are around 13 bars in the House of Commons – enough to cover every possible eventuality in the life of an MP.

There are bars for passing on secrets, bars for impressing the Secretary of your

more active than the men they drag around with them, bombarding Members of Parliament with resolutions passed in the Women's Section and threatening deselection, if not castration, should their Parliamentary Representative fail to meet their demands or – far worse! – hint that he in any way regards women as female.

THE FAR LEFT

Paradoxically, though, the farther Left you go, the less everything from scandal to sexual proclivities matter. The kind of people who become the most ardent activists not only have no interest at all in the Member's marital state but, further, frequently feel that unorthodox sexual orientation is a positive mark in his favour, striking as it does a blow for minority interests of all kinds.

LIBERAL

It is very difficult indeed to think of a Liberal member in terms of sexual achievement, largely because the Party's whole amatory history makes it such nervous work. Liberal members tend to hunch up defensively against the past, the twin shadows of Lloyd George and the Thorpe scandal peering as it were over their shoulders; and this uneasiness inevitably gives the impression that they aren't sure if they have got it all together.

S.D.P.

Love in the S.D.P., on the other hand, is a sensible, frequent and thoroughly mature activity, with nothing of the Tory Party's behind-the-scenes secretiveness nor the Labour member's brisk bang-and-off-to-the-next-

Militant-meeting. But just as one of the S.D.P.'s besetting sins is their overwhelmingly bureaucratic method of arriving at decisions, with nothing left to chance or inspiration and everything down in triplicate, so there is no getting at it until both of you have sat down and talked about the whole thing throughly, responsibly and maturely, with everything from the date, time and place of the next meeting to whether or not it's worth having a vasectomy discussed in orderly fashion. Then love, accompanied by a bottle of claret and followed by a good book, takes place (in triplicate, naturally). The healthy sex lives of S.D.P. members are yet another compelling argument for proportional representation.

P·A·I·R·I·N·G O·F·F

For the MP to do any real-life pairing off it is essential for him to have a pair – a fellow MP on the opposite side with whom he can mutually agree either absence or presence so that the Government's majority isn't affected.

Great care should be exercised in the choice of partner in this vital relationship – of far greater durability and importance than any transient liaison – for without an amenable pair, the MP may be confined to the Palace of Westminster night after

night, moping disconsolately as his fellows set off for life and love in the great world beyond.

The ideal pair is Eric Heffer, who spends every spare evening talking Marxism to four besandalled primary school teachers in Islington.

local Party, bars for being with members of your own Party, bars for getting away from members of your own Party, bars that act as a decompression chamber between the MP and the outside world – here, Ministers can be recognised by the speed with which they down a few quick revivers before dashing off to their next appointment. And last but not least, there are bars for taking women with whom you have, or hope to have, a meaningful relationship.

In the popular Strangers' Bar, middle-aged MPs are quite often seen with young women who may or may not be their nieces. Forward lady journalists ask MPs to the Press Bar. There is also another Press Bar, called Annie's (many House of Commons bars are named after barmaids, who are often but a dim folk memory) where the only kind of adulterous affair possible is with a member of the Parliamentary Lobby – this, naturally, is known as an in-depth off-the-record briefing. The best bar for entertaining mistresses to dinner is undoubtedly the Harcourt Room – prettier, quieter, more romantic and more expensive than the Strangers' Dining Room upstairs. This, with its faint overtones of Paddington Station that hint at the need for brisk and punctual departure, is ideally suited to elderly aunts and constituents of the less welcome kind.

The terrace

The Terrace is every MP's secret weapon, not simply for its prestige but for its beauty. Even on the most sultry day there is a breeze; the wide panoramic view changes constantly; and the endless to-and-froing of the busy river traffic has an effect somewhat akin to that of watching goldfish in your dentist's waiting room – i.e., subliminally relaxing. In other words, the Terrace is a place where even the wariest may momentarily drop their defences, a phenomenon

> ❝ *The Terrace is a place where even the wariest may momentarily drop their defences* ❞

that becomes ever more apparent as the day draws on. On balmy summer evenings, the ratio of successful approaches must be something of a national record: everyone is off duty, Members are just hanging around waiting for the vote, and drink is circulating freely. As the night wears on, to sit Pimms in hand in the warm June dusk, while the stars emerge one by one and the Finance Bill crawls on its stupefying way inside is not only idyllically romantic but tinged with that sense of the exotic and forbidden which has proved many a maiden's downfall.

Where and when

The Honourable Member's Parliamentary day does not officially start until the afternoon. Mornings are generally devoted by

ON A CLEAR NIGHT YOU CAN SEE THE GLOW FROM THE BEDROOM OF MY PENTHOUSE FLAT

FOOT STEPS

When deeply moved, older MPs sometimes resort to the Michael Foot school of punctuation ('I cannot tell you how much your. Support means to me at this. Crucial moment in our national history') both in public and in private ('I cannot tell you how much your. Support means to me at this. Crucial moment in my personal history'); younger ones to blazing eyes and a little manly incoherence.

Conservative MPs to making money, by Labour MPs to making speeches and by the S.D.P., it is enviously believed, to making love. Many MPs, of course, are on the Committees of some sort, but even these can provide the perfect alibi. Who is to know for sure whether you are on the Select Committee for the Environment off to Dounreay next week to look at a reactor? Still less, who cares?

But as a rendezvous for assignations there is little to touch the House of Commons itself, with its marvellously romantic atmosphere that plays on the emotions of susceptible young women – and into the MP's hand. At night, especially, its effect is overwhelming. 'If you go in somewhere between 10 and 11, when everyone is dispersing, it's a terribly private, incredibly romantic place,' says one girl. 'All that grey stone, half lit, those miles and miles of corridor and of course the associations . . .'

The physical conditions for romance have also improved over recent years. Where, once, MPs and secretaries shared crowded offices or worked in a corner of the corridor, today many MPs have their own offices – complete with carpets, door keys and net curtains on the window. Even the furniture could have been designed to make relationships easier: now there are large sofas and comfortable Habitat-type chairs with large foot-pouffe extensions.

For those Westminster couples who prefer to conduct their romance in the even greater privacy of the flat owned by one or other, the hundreds of different entrances and exits to the House of Commons make it possible to avoid that notorious giveaway: the joint departure. 'Can I offer you a lift home?' says the MP. 'I'll just get my car – oh, by the way, you might as well go out by the Lords'.

The away match

But all these everyday shifts and stratagems pale into insignificance beside that gateway to romance known as Parliamentary Service Abroad. Just as publishing has its Book Fairs, journalism its travel freebies and the academic world its Conferences, so Parliamentary life has the Council of Europe, the North Atlantic Assembly and the Western European Union. The fortunate MP invited by the Whips to serve on one of these non-elected bodies at the taxpayer's expense is sent to Strasbourg, Paris or somewhere as joyously far-flung as San Francisco. As the plane flies out, a holiday atmosphere takes over, glasses are raised and the handout bottles of *Ma Griffe* slid into pockets, later to be presented judiciously to the most personable of the waiting corps of interpreters. In the event of the MP not striking lucky, these bottles will be brought back as evidence that loved ones were never far from his mind even while he was wearily toiling in foreign parts – and oh! how he wishes he had been. For almost as potent as the unalloyed fragrance of 35 phials of the same perfume rising from the bodies of the interpreters is the scent of lost youth that hangs over the whole proceedings.

10 Love in Fleet Street

J ust about every aspect of love in Fleet Street is governed by the clock. Diary editors stagger back to their typewriters after a steamy session to write a new lead for the next edition, news editors disentangle themselves from convoluted embraces (in Fleet Street, only ecclesiastical correspondents avail themselves of the missionary position) at precisely one minute to the hour in order to switch on the radio news bulletin.

Deadline dating

It is also fast. In an industry where Forward Planning means tomorrow and affairs have to be fitted in between editions, nobody thinks in terms of the long siege. But despite the speed at which liaisons ignite, they often last for years for the same reason: neither party has a spare minute to find someone else.

Mostly, love in Fleet Street is geared to the hours Fleet Street works. Daily papers offer the greatest flexibility; with a working day that starts any time after ten and can stretch until midnight or after if you want it to, there is an excuse for every day of the week except Saturday. Evening papers are a trifle trickier for potential lovers, with little

Yes, but has it been libelised?

OPENING GAMBITS

... In the office

- I liked your piece/photograph/page in yesterday's paper.

- I gather we're both going to the Quartet party – shall we share a cab?

- Was it you who wrote that marvellous piece on Jerry Hall?

- How do you spell iatrogenic?

- It's time we had lunch.

- Come and split a bottle of champagne.

... and outside it

- So you're interested in becoming a journalist?

- There's a piece in that, you know.

- You mean you've never seen round a newspaper office?

- I'll introduce you to our Picture Editor.

- What about slipping out to see the first edition printed – we can always come back to the party later.

- D'you like the Caprice, or is there somewhere else you prefer?

each other's wives. Occasionally, this course is pursued more as a matter of getting back at a disliked colleague than simple lust; the risk here is that if the colleague gets promoted he may get his cuckolder transferred to Manchester.

But the intellectual seriousness of any given newspaper is no guarantee of high moral fibre among the staff (although the converse is invariably true). Newspapers have an outsize dollop of the two well-known British traits of hypocrisy and sentimentality. They will launch funds to *Send a Sick Kiddie to The Seaside,* yet when the coach crashes on the Saturday evening journey back the first thing anyone says is a wistful 'What a story for the Sundays!' And there are few prettier sights in the world than a Back Bench with a dozen assorted wives, ex-wives, and mistresses between them, not to speak of a couple of bastards, debating the right headline with which to castigate the moral delinquency of some Minister.

Not surprisingly, there are gender differences galore. In the picture that appears beside their byline, male writers look stern, brooding, idealistic, even menacing, but female columnists have to look happy and fulfilled, which means A Smile. (Female writers' photographs, incidentally, cause

> **66** *Fleet Street's best performances are always against deadlines* **99**

or no ostensible reason for staying in the office after 5.30 (see Parties); and though the more leisurely pace of the Sundays is theoretically promising, it also slows down the tempo of the affair itself. Fleet Street's best performances are always against deadlines.

This of course affects venue. While affairs on the quality Sundays (and to a certain extent the more upmarket dailies) tend to rumble round the dinner tables of N.1., in the tabloids it's usually the office – the Mirror in particular being a hotbed of romance. Indeed, so incestuous are some offices that even the subs have affairs with

almost more trouble than anything else on a newspaper; one woman columnist is notorious for the thousands she cost her paper in working through every major photographer before finding a shot with which she was grudgingly satisfied.)

Otherwise, newspapers care little what a woman does as long as she's not embarrassing. She is given maternity leave when she has a baby by a senior and married male member of the staff; she can dress outrageously, get drunk at the Christmas party,

bring her dogs, cats or children into the office every day as long as she is reasonably discreet and turns her copy in on time.

For women, most Fleet Street affairs are doomed to failure. For most, the long, irregular and anti-social hours mean little reliable social life outside the office; and the men they see long enough to fall in love with are colleagues, who by the time they have achieved Fleet Street from the provinces usually have wives and young children at home whom they have no intention of leaving.

Fleet Street is also physically and psychologically tough on women, who find it more difficult to take the long hours, let alone the constant drinking and the equally incessant politicking, and then go home to an empty flat. Some girls go right through the office, chalking up married man after married man. The reason there is so much sex in Fleet Street is that it is full of people who spend long hours late at night doing very little but who live too far away to go home

between editions; at the same time, there are sudden spurts of frantic action that cause the adrenalin to churn. 'Producing a newspaper gives you a sense of power over the daily events of life, which is a tremendous turn-on' sums up one executive. 'In other words, you feel very randy.'

But suddenly there is a panic. The newspaper is bought by a new proprietor, the editor changes, there are rumours of shutdown or redundancy – and the incidence of affairs drops sharply. It is only when Fleet Street people *worry* about their jobs that they stop thinking about sex.

The Cast
The Photographer

Undoubtedly the randiest journalist in the business is the Fleet Street photographer. Aggressively heterosexual (almost all staff photographers are male) he regards any photograph of an attractive woman not taken from pavement level and as near her feet as possible as a failure (with Royalty, this is translated into waiting for hours on the sidelines on a chilly day until the moment the wind fleetingly whisks up the august skirts).

Keeping the score

Many photographers look like walking advertisements for *A Good Time,* in skin-tight jeans, leather jackets and phallic-looking cameras with ten-inch lenses slung low round their necks to point forward suggestively; although these aren't always the ones to beware of. Photographers who work on the show business side tend to do best; one famous writer-photographer team used to keep a joint score chart and if one or other of them didn't score during or after the interview, a cloud was cast over the day.

Photographers also have first pick of all the little model girls who want to get their picture in the paper (to be fair, the photographer always tries and usually succeeds in

EXCUSES

As love in Fleet Street takes place almost exclusively within working hours, two sets of excuses are needed: for the office, and for those who may be expecting you at home or elsewhere.

At the office, far and away the commonest pretext for a sudden dart to the beloved's side is the magic phrase 'I'm going to have my hair cut'. A quick glance round any newspaper office will produce at least one executive whose hair is always noticeably trim, never developing that needs-a-haircut look, the reason being, of course, the hair-cutting takes place on an almost daily basis.

Here are some more favourites:
- I'll be out on location   (*Fashion editor, fashion photographer*)
- I'm having a drink with a contact   (*Anyone*)
- I'm having a drink in the Whips' Office   (*Lobby correspondent*)
- I've got to go to a screening/ rehearsal/preview (*Anyone on the film, arts or TV side*)
- I'm going up to the Sixth Floor   (*Editor*)

keeping his side of the bargain). The only thing photographers have to beware of is going to bed with female journalists: when one famous lensman laid two well-known women columnists in brisk succession, embarrassing details of his physical under-endowment in certain respects were all round Fleet Street in what you might call a flash.

The Journalist

Certain journalists are open to sexual brib-ery, notably film, showbiz and gossip columnists ('it isn't the debs but their Mums who want to get you into bed so that you'll publicise their darling daughters'). What-ever their behaviour, few dare put the finger on the gossip columnist spotted weekend-ing with a comely blonde at that delightful Oxford hotel, Le Manoir aux Quat'Saisons for fear of what he will do to them in his subsequent column.

While most Fleet Street love is in-Street if not in-house, there are of course excep-tions (and the first thing anyone con-templating an affair outside Fleet Street does is check their intended in the cuttings). Fashion editors – apart from those for whom 'fashion' means saucy underwear var-ied by revealing swimsuits or diaphanous negligée offers – are a breed of their own,

'His jacket's still here.'

Fleet Street is possibly the only profes-sion where a simple everyday article of outerwear is the perfect alibi. A jacket slung over the back of your chair is the accepted sign that even though your physical body may not be present at that moment you are, actually, *there*. Hence the invariable answer to any enquiry except the most urgent: 'He's around somewhere – his jacket's still here'. Pressed further, the colleague at the next desk will mutter that you must be down on the stone, in some far corner, in the canteen, slipped out for a quick one, closeted with the Editor or getting cut-tings from the Library (this one is good for hours in most newspapers). Profes-sional absentees always order two jackets for each suit, leaving one on the chair-back and putting on the other when they go for a quick wash and brush up before setting out for an evening's revelry. Only when they forget to move credit cards or latchkeys of the nearby lovenest from one to the other does Nemesis strike.

"Few use sex to get a better interview"

sitting in small enclaves filled with pot plants off the main office, dowered with more help than anyone except the editor and given to copy like *Think Landed Gentry This Winter*. Most are recruited from glossy magazines and lead a perfectly normal life outside the office.

Literary editors shade off into the world of books, becoming entangled with publishers, authors and, most likely of all, reviewers. A lot of women writers become fleetingly or permanently involved with the man they have been sent to interview and, in some cases, never return to the office. Few use sex to get a better interview, though one is notorious for putting a tape recorder under the bed when it does occur. Top Fleet Street women, on the other hand, tend to be married to men in Fleet Street, as they are the only ones who will understand their way of life.

WHO WITH

Affairs between colleagues (that is, someone who holds a card to the same union as yourself) are commonest, though secretaries are often considered the traditional preserve of the Back Bench, and editors and Chairmen sometimes marry theirs (the editor who merely has an affair with his is locked into a close but often uneasy alliance for the rest of his working life). For women the reverse does not apply: the lady writer or executive can have a toyboy but not a copyboy.

The Night Editor

Second only to the dictatorship of the clock, love in Fleet Street hinges on three important factors. Two of these are the *Jacket* and the *Telephone*; the third is the *Night Editor*.

The ideal candidate for this key post is a man of tact, discretion, loyalty, the ability to size up a situation instantly, and possibly even a flair for news. For most of the night hours everything is in his hands and anything outside the normal course of work will be referred to him. So if a telephone call comes through for a senior executive from wife, mistress, estranged mistress, would-be girl friend or even by some mischance the Proprietor himself, it is the Night Editor who fields it.

He must, therefore, be expert at instantly recognising the tone of the conversation and then making the right response. These are:

- He is out with the ambassador
- Oh, it's you
- He has been called to Downing Street
- He's round the corner having a drink at the Press Club but I'm afraid you won't get him there as he just rang to say he is on his way back
- Can I take a message, Sir, as he will be ringing in any moment?

The next move, naturally, is for the Night Editor to reach first into his hip pocket for the slip of paper on which are written the telephone numbers at which various wandering executives can be reached during the night, then for the nearest direct outside line, to utter in a neutral tone of voice the time-honoured phrase 'John, something's cropped up at the office and I think it needs your personal attention.'

Getting away from it all

Freebies of all kinds, including and especially travel trips, are the most obvious method, although they have the disadvantage that you are operating not only under the eye of fellow hacks but that of the PR who has arranged the trip, who may well refer inconsequentially to one of your wilder moments next time she rings up to plead for a little editorial. And although it is widely considered that once past the white cliffs of Dover anything goes in the way of conduct or expenses, once back home it will all be related for the delectation of colleagues, friends and enemies.

The most successful practitioners operate singly (well, in pairs) using a foolproof excuse. What this is depends largely on rank. Editors can visit New York to case out new photosetting techniques or jaunt off to Blackpool at conference time to renew old contacts, though even here the best-laid (and I use the word advisedly) plans can go wrong – one editor suffered a heart attack in mid-contact renewal, though fortunately his paramour was the paper's Medical Correspondent. For others reasonably high up in the hierarchy a visit to the Manchester office is a good pretext (often also used when there is a Test Match at Old Trafford); while preprint colour offers an excellent chance for sampling some small but congenial country hotel – most plant is in places like Liverpool or Peterborough and a quick telephone call to a friendly printer contact there will ensure you have the right information to make your excuse for a visit realistic.

For one particular type of journalist, the Foreign Correspondent, the world, amorously speaking, is his oyster. This is because no Foreign Desk has any idea of geography, accepting unquestioningly the proposition that the quickest way to reach Durban is via Los Angeles, so that it is perfectly possible to visit a loved one in New York, Rome, Paris or any other city with a major airport at least once a fortnight.

For anyone else, these little sorties, however carefully planned and whether or not in office hours, *must* be accompanied by

Printers are seldom sex objects.

a foolproof reason for being there. Otherwise Sod's Law takes over; and in the remote Provençal village the two of you find the Cycling Correspondent as he waits for the Tour de France to pass. A friend of mine once flew to Paris for lunch and an afternoon of love – needless to say, the first person she and her lover ran into as they strolled arm-in-arm down the Bois towards their hotel was a member of the paper's gossip column team. Many people simply give up the struggle for secrecy, remarking 'Oh, didn't you know about *us?*' After all, they reason, no story lasts longer than a week.

The Wife

Another familiar characteristic of love in Fleet Street is the stormy intervention of the wronged wife. Sometimes, when an affair has been coasting along for so many months everyone else has lost interest, the wife finds out; perhaps through a telling reference in Private Eye, perhaps through a half-completed expense sheet accompanied by a bill

featuring room service for two, perhaps by an incautious telephone call. Next thing, she is in the pub tearing at her rival's hair, sneaking into the office car park and scraping rude messages on the side of her husband's company car, in the office conning his secretary into handling over his contact book (later to be burnt or shredded) or – if she happens to be in Fleet Street herself – bursting into print in rival papers. Articles by a wronged wife can always be recognised by the fact that, whatever the subject, it is dragged round to contain a scathing reference to the moral lacunae of her erstwhile spouse ('and talking of men, the worst kind of rat is one who . . .').

Where it happens

Inevitably, the Strand Palace Hotel (only a quick bus ride from the office and no big expense). Those who reach executive status usually try for something more imaginative; a suite at the Savoy is considered glamorous but risky – too many editors lunch or dine there – so the Ritz, though less convenient, is safer. Small hotels such as Great Fosters at Egham are deservedly popular among those who can find a suitable pretext for spending a large part of the night away. Note: it is a sensible precaution to route any return journey via the office. Anyone who staggers through their front door clutching a copy of next day's paper stamped with the

---

E X C U S E S   F O R

B E I N G   L A T E   H O M E

- It's A's farewell party.

- B is getting married so we're all having a drink.

- C's been made up to Assistant Editor so we're all having a drink.

- D's book is published today so we're having a quick drink at El Vino's.

- It's F's birthday so he's buying us a quick drink at El Vino's.

- Everyone else is out getting drunk so I'm stuck here.

word *Voucher* in red has clearly been working hard at the office all night.

Often, this is not too far from the truth, for sometimes love takes place within the office itself, generally after an evening's drinking and because even in open-plan offices there are endless nooks and crannies. Equally, however late the hour, someone is always around, if not the Security Officer then the cleaner; many are the stories of

at their liveliest between seven and ten in the evening – that is, between the first and third editions. Traditionally, the most desirable locations are the Inns of Court, usually deserted by then and near enough to the office to make both love and dinner possible. Most popular are Lincoln's Inn Fields and the Gray's Inn Road; though at the Sunday Times opinions are divided on the latter, extreme closeness to the office (good)

THE TELEPHONE

The necessity of always being at the end of a telephone is a major complication of love in Fleet Street. Wherever you are, whether you are working or officially off duty, you must leave a number from which you can be reeled in like a fish on a line if need be.

Nevertheless, it is important to maintain a certain degree of mystery as to your whereabouts, if only for the excellent psychological reason that the less anyone can picture your private

life, the more reluctant they are to disturb you at it. Thus when you leave that evening's telephone number, never say where you are going but remark simply: 'I can be reached at 123 45678'.

Rule Two is never to allow your lover to answer the telephone even if you are in the bath; on that occasion it won't be Room Service but your spouse, to whom a thick or jealous colleague has passed on your number. With a regular liaison, the most sensible of all investments is an answerphone that broadcasts the caller's message, giving you a few moments to frame a suitable reply or excuse before ringing back.

---

couples being locked in store cupboards for the night or thrown into spasm by the sudden springing into life of an industrial Hoover the other side of a partition. The cleaners themselves take such things in their stride. 'Don't move, Sir' said one who came into a Deputy Editor's office to find him sprawled across the desk top with a pretty lady sub-editor. 'I'll dust round you.'

The Love Nest

Many of those in the top salary and expenses bracket and with a longish journey home can put forward a convincing argument as to the need for a small *pied-à-terre* near Fleet Street. These dwellings are often

weighing against being spotted by a colleague (bad).

The building of the Barbican, halfway between Fleet Street and the City, provides a new and much-needed source of such *garçonnières*, especially for the City Editor ('I'm just off to see my contacts at Rothschilds'). Many of those in management are already following this trend, but what will happen over the next few years as the advent of new technology forces a move eastward into Dockland is anybody's guess.

❝ *Don't move, Sir.*
I'll dust round you ❞

SAYINGS
of the week

Many newspapers have a section headed *Sayings of the Week*.
Here are a few Sayings you can hear *inside* a newspaper
on any ordinary week.

- If you really want to know, the reason I'm late back is because
  I got absolutely paralytic at lunch time.

- Let's have lunch, and we can discuss your contribution to the paper.

- He put his arm round my waist but I didn't move it because I might
  want to shift departments and he *is* the Deputy Editor.

- I could get hold of the office car, you know.

- You're wasting your money, old boy. I happen to know
  she only does it in lifts.

I'M SORRY, BUT THE DEPUTY EDITOR IS SHACKED UP WITH SOME FLOOSIE IN HIS KNIGHTSBRIDGE FLAT THIS AFTERNOON

Paying for it

If alcohol often triggers affairs, expenses are the power packs that keep them going, with the courtship lunch set down as *To Entertaining House of Commons Press Officer, Bill Attached*, and anything from champagne, flowers, taxis or a bottle of scent hidden under the magic word *Contacts*.

Because there is such a fine line between what is allowable (i.e., what is tacitly regarded as the rate for the job) and what isn't, managements still do not regard fiddling expenses on even the most dramatic scale as anything like as serious as, say, belonging to the Socialist Workers' Party. True, people have been fired for what in any other organisation would be a matter for the police (one man used to sign and claim a regular weekly fictitious sheet for £400) but most are promptly taken on by other papers, and the oft-repeated story about the late James Cameron is regarded as a witty way of putting those smart-alecs in Accounts in their place rather than sharp practice.

Clever-dick accountant to Mr Cameron, newly returned from a middle east trip: 'Mr Cameron, it says here on your expenses, *To Purchase of Camel, £200.* How can you justify this?'

CAMERON: 'It was the only way across the desert.'

ACCOUNTANT, triumphantly: 'Well, then, *where is the camel?*'

CAMERON, writing: 'Oh, sorry, I forgot this.' The added line read: *To Burial of Camel, £300.*

SILENCE IS . . . *unknown*

People in Fleet Street who have affairs always think nobody else knows, but in fact everyone does; it is simply considered not polite to let on that you do. There is a faint chance of keeping at least the details secret if

How the nitty-gritty passes round Fleet Street.

you tell no one, but if even one person is told under the blackest oath of secrecy the whole thing is out*. Fleet Street people consider that if you are in the business of communication keeping secrets smacks of unnatural practices; as for learning them, anyone who can find out what happened in Downing Street yesterday certainly knows what's going on two desks away.

*Not for nothing is the Mirror pub familiarly known as The Stab (short, of course, for Stab in the Back).

The break up

The first sign of a Fleet Street affair coming to an end is when the woman concerned comes in to the office wearing dark glasses (the nearest most people get to a room of their own) behind which she can hide the ravages of a tearstained night while progressing with that day's piece on *How to Succeed With Men*. As a rule of thumb, the blacker the glasses, the deeper the emotional crisis.

While many amorous bouts are really no more than the combined results of adrenalin, hanging around and an evening's alcohol, and leave no more trace than a vague afterglow of friendliness, in cases of love that goes wrong (and indeed, often of love that goes right), there is only one rule: the woman always leaves.

> 'A triumph of mind is often only overmatter'.
>
> HAROLD EVANS

11 Love in Television

Television people give an impression of reading magazines rather than books, combined with a sense of belief in their own high moral calling to publish the truth and cleanse the world of lies (thus they hated Nixon more than Brezhnev: Brezhnev merely tortured people to death but Nixon tried to fool the media). Inside the industry there are similar dichotomies: those who thrust or hustle to get in front of the cameras as presenters or interviewers are despised ever so slightly by the producers; and there is a sharp split in attitude between those with staff jobs and those who work on contract (in practice, all the creative ones). This is because everyone on the financial side basically distrusts creative people – who may occasionally land them with a dud programme – and exacerbated by the fact that many executives like to see themselves as power brokers, uttering a godlike 'I'll take you on for a year and see how things go'. Like Victorian husbands, TV bosses believe that only by keeping creative people in a state of feeling permanently threatened and slightly on edge, will they give of their best. As only the very few

manage to climb out of the Whickerwork into an impregnable position, it is almost needless to say that the principle of *Never Let Them Get Settled* makes creative people twice as neurotic, and many resort to faster spending, harder drinking and wilder love affairs to compensate.

Sometimes these affairs are with one of a special breed of dedicated woman found in television who focuses all her devotion on one man. For this senior editor or producer she will work long and antisocial hours, give up her weekend or spend Sunday on a slow train to Sunderland with a batch of scripts under her arm without a second's thought, long after the man concerned has shouted 'Cut!' on the affair itself.

There are only two things you can get sacked for at the BBC: one is not paying your licence fee and the other is having a serious and public affair with a superior (or inferior) in the same department which could cause charges of favouritism to be levelled. The first people to challenge the system were Esther Rantzen and Desmond Willcox. They subsequently married – but the ban on unpaid licences still exists.

The pioneers

Morning stars

Even among media people, TV am is famous for the freedom and inventiveness of its various romantic intrigues, which invest it with an aura of sexual licence unknown outside its custom-built walls. Under the four egg-cups, couples, not to speak of coupling, are very common. This is partly due to the setting: the beautiful mod-ern offices from which the lapping of the canal can be heard and the rooms fringed with palms have something of the air of an exotic resort, putting the idea of holiday romance subliminally into everyone's heads; partly it is due to the siege mentality of the majority of those in the company – possibly the only place left where idealistic pro-gramme makers still believe they can change the face of British television.

OPENING GAMBITS

MOST PRESENTERS LOOK MUCH LESS GLAMOROUS OFF-SCREEN

★ Opening gambit from producer to production secretary: We've got to go through timings on those interviews tonight so we know how much we've got in the can by tomorrow. Your room or mine?

★ Opening gambit from director to actress: We've got to work through that tricky bit where Joe discovers you in his bed before we move on to Act II tomorrow. Your flat or mine?

★ Opening gambit from actress to cameraman: You said you'd see if backlighting disguised the bump in my nose. I've got an hour before my next shot. Your caravan or mine?

★ Opening gambit from scriptwriter to production assistant: You look as though you could do with a drink. I've got a bottle of scotch. Your place or mine?

Tribalisation

Love in television is largely influenced by geographical considerations. Not only is the maze-like interior of Broadcasting House prohibitive of romance – even people who have worked there 10 or 15 years get lost on the way to their offices – but there are built-in barriers to meeting people at regular hours. Departments in every TV company are not only separate but frequently physically apart as well, with the result that relationships are tribalised, with liaisons occurring only within the Department. Fortunately, a considerable number of permutations are possible. Here is a handy guide to some of them.

Camera crews are almost totally male, except for the Vision Mixer, who is usually happily married, 45–50, and living in Pinner; and therefore not an erotic focus

except, presumably, for Mr Vision Mixer. Most cameramen are good working class lads who drink a prodigious amount of beer, give off a strong 'out with the boys' aura, and have wives and children tucked away in the suburbs. They always travel first class and everyone, from the studio bosses to the director on the set, places a great premium on keeping the cameraman and lighting man happy. So, quite often, does the female lead: actresses go for cameramen sometimes because they make them look so good, sometimes because they fancy a bit of rough.

In *News,* everyone is basically a journalist (with a strand of civil servant, in the case of those belonging to the BBC). Television journalists are characterised by great articulacy and an ability not only to think on their feet but capitalise on any situation – while being eaten alive by piranha fish, most could give a fluent and fascinating commentary on how it felt. They tend to belong to the *Wham Bam Thank you Ma'am* school of amorists, picking up love where they find it – though preferring to describe this process as 'snatching a few brief moments of happiness'. Those with a foreign beat frequently turn up unexpectedly a couple of years after the beloved concerned has last seen them and usually succeed in skilfully evoking a sentimental stroll down Memory Lane 'for old times' sake'.

Producers are both full of themselves to the point of arrogance and terribly anxious (if they are also the director these two traits are even more noticeable). Producers fall in

Production assistants can usually be found at the producer's side, though often this position changes dramatically.

love with female presenters – the goodlooking, young female presenter is the most sought-after figure in TV – for the simple reason that the producer, in attempting to hire a young woman whom all the men out there will fancy, naturally hires someone he himself fancies. Falling headlong into the trap he has dug, he does everything he can to further her career and, if she hides an ambitious mind behind her perfect brow, before you can say 'Hello, Welcome and Good Evening', she's using him more than he's using her.

Directors are much more quote, artistic, unquote, and will talk of their Art with enviable fluency for hours at a time. They

too describe what it feels like to be eaten alive by piranha fish, only in their case they are referring to Accounts (or the producer, Department Head or whoever is being unsympathetic to their budgetary or artistic needs of the moment). Directors and actresses are a natural pairing, a symbiotic relationship that involves her placing herself in his hands for the duration of the drama, his guiding her to the best possible performance, which does not always take place on the set.

Production assistants, whose expertise with clipboard, stopwatch and typewriter is invaluable to the producer, are almost always female. But while assistant producers

❝ Isn't she wonderful? You know, I couldn't have made the film without her! ❞

often rise to become producers, production assistant is often the female cut-off level. One well-known way out of this career cul-de-sac is via an affair with an influential producer. So when a producer says on the team's return from filming on location: *'Isn't she wonderful? You know, I couldn't have made the film without her!'*, everyone knows that a lot more than the film has been made.

Drama is rooted in the theatre, with actors and often directors hired for specific productions and theatre-like atmosphere surrounding even the Department's offices. Actors and actresses who meet at the studio often have intense, briefish affairs with each other which invariably go wrong just before

one of them is due on the set. The consequent shouted recriminations turn the director's hair white as he listens to cries of 'I LOVE YOU, you silly bitch!' hurled after the female lead as she runs down the stairs in tears 30 seconds before the red light goes on.

Comedy and *Variety* are rather like drama in their use of outside writers and actors but have a far heavier reliance on agents and are thus full of agent-jokes. They barter over percentages, introductions, favours, rights, royalties and the unloading of four lesser artistes the studio doesn't want in return for getting them the big star they have to have. Naturally, much of the currency is sexual.

Further education is full of people terribly proud of what they are doing on the one hand but desperately anxious to get into mainstream TV on the other; their characteristic expression is one of high-minded conflict.

Current affairs and *documentaries,* where most of the permanent staff are to be found, are the focus of most of the aggressiveness floating round any television company. At the lower levels, staff are split roughly half and half, male and female, so partnerships spring up overnight.

I'm afraid I'm going to be terribly late home because:

- We've lost a whole interview and we're searching the cutting room for it.
- Trevor wants to see his film before we cut it and he can only make nine o'clock tonight.
- Blast it, we've wiped a whole section of videotape and we've got to do a retransfer.

The Television Ego

For anyone from 'outside' contemplating an affair with a TV person, one lesser-known hazard is the Television Ego. This can be summed up as a belief that television is what the world revolves around and those fortunate enough to have their homes invaded or questions like 'And how did you feel when you saw your family drown before your eyes, Mrs Smith?' posed ten minutes after the disaster, should count themselves among the blessed of the earth. It should be noted that the BBC version of the Ego, though less flamboyant than its manifestations on the commercial channels, is marginally more arrogant, partly because of the folk memory of the halcyon days when the Beeb was the only channel, partly because of a strong sense of moral imperative regarding the sacred role of the BBC as communicator, truth-purveyor, etc.

conditions here are not conductive to serious romancing. There are too many people you know crammed cheek by jowl and, with everyone wearing a name badge, even those you don't will have no trouble identifying you later on. With every single major company in the world represented,

D · R · I · N · K

One school of thought claims that the drink after work is really part of work: you're still talking about the programme but after four gin and tonics you say what you *really* think. Because of occasional disasters on the air, it is the BBC's policy not to provide spirits

in the famed Hospitality Room and most guests are too nervous to drink much anyway. Production people are equally nervous but as they don't have to appear, no such inhibition constrains them. The result is that after the programme there is a sense of relief

and abandon which provides a fertile starting-point for affairs. Guests go off into the night two by two, rather in the spirit of those descending from the Ark having survived the hazards of the Flood, with Noah's injunction to *Go Forth and Multiply* ringing in their ears.

Internally, the Television Ego is an enormously motivating force, hence those names that unroll endlessly on the screen after even the briefest sitcom ('If she won't do it for the money, offer her a credit'). When two television persons get together, both of them know the initial stages of courtship are not so much a ritual dance as a jockeying for position; but for the unwary outsider, the first encounter with the Ego can have the force and irreversibility of an unexpected meeting with a hungry python.

Away from it all

Just as publishing has its book fairs and the academic world its conferences and summer schools, so television people have their annual feast of Misrule, more commonly known as the Edinburgh Festival. For although the industry's greatest official get together is the television market MIP, (the Marché Internationale de Programmes de Télévision), held every spring in Cannes,

no one wants to blot their copybook; with a registration fee of £400 and dinner in even a one-star restaurant £70 a head, the accent is on business results rather than pleasure. Besides, in early May it's too cold for the girls to go topless. So although a certain amount of action takes place on the terrace of the Carlton and in hotel bars, where sales assistants and secretaries make a Perrier last the whole evening while waiting for Mr Wrong, the buyer for King Kong videos, to make his approach, on the whole MIP means making deals rather than being made.

Although Edinburgh has only been a television festival for about six years, it is where all the industry's serious extra-marital activity now takes place. As everyone in a position to do so automatically awards themselves a week in Edinburgh as a coda to their summer holidays, no meaningful decision is ever made about any television programme between June and September. After a short lull to recover from the excesses of both, the wheels start to whirr in late

WELL
– WHY NOT?

Filming trips are the byword launch pad for affairs, especially for the production assistant who is often the only female on them. Sometimes girls start an affair with one man simply to ward off the attentions of all the others, a reaction made even more natural by the general assumption that location is open season and anything goes. Rather like being abroad on a school trip, there is the feeling that you have lost your identity for the duration, and with it all constraints, a feeling of unreality heightened by the fact that the money you're spending isn't your own. In the networks, this attitude is often part of everyday life, since many of those who work in the regions commute from their homes in London to a weekday pad in Manchester, Birmingham or Yorkshire and a local liaison.

October when the clocks change to mark the end of Summer Time in all senses of the word.

While everyone agrees that being away from home without the hampering presence of loved ones or the need to justify expenditure in terms of work done accounts for the atmosphere of joyous abandon prevalent from the moment of boarding the night sleeper, there are two distinct approaches to the question of where best to base yourself.

Hotels are considered nem. con. too banal, not to speak of too visible; many thoughtful companies, like LWT and Euston Films block-book flats a year in advance so that their executives can be assured of the necessary privacy. Others prefer to stay on campus, reliving their Sixties undergraduate days of protest marches, sit-ins and the heady spring of the Permissive Society. Add in the comforting knowledge that the whole thing is designed as a gigantic tax loss, with no one paying personally for so much as the initial drink, and it is little wonder that in the television industry Edinburgh, rather than Paris, is known as the Capital of Love.

GOING THROUGH THE … MOTIONS

Television is probably the only industry where it is not necessarily incriminating if the producer's wife rings up the hotel in Sunderland where the producer is staying, and the producer's beautiful secretary answers the telephone in his bedroom at midnight. What they are doing, you see, is going through that day's tapes, which has to be done before next morning's shooting, because if anything has gone wrong then it will have to be done again before moving on to the next part of the shooting schedule. Anyhow, that's their story.

Clothes

Clothes worn by television people serve not only to project the requisite image but also give a clear pointer as to how they see themselves. Since many TV affairs are designed to further careers, clothes can be a valuable guide to who to home in on.

Technicians and camera crews wear expensive Sergio Tacchini-type leisurewear and Nike trainers, young female Oxford graduates sport straight pageboys, men's shirts and floppy jumpers, serious television directors have Neil Kinnock haircuts and wear their battered leather jackets everywhere including, it is popularly believed, bed. ITV company men wear shirts and ties but producers in other independent companies stick to shirts they bought in Honolulu, paired with anything from sandals to combat boots. Writers can be spotted because they are usually the worst dressed of all, while sunglasses provide the perfect cover for both sexes to size each other up without being seen to do so. Most important indicator of all, however, is . . .

The production teeshirt

Long before a series actually goes into production, somebody walks in wearing a teeshirt saying 'I'm in BLOTT ON THE LANDSCAPE', and a great buzz of envy and desire goes round the studio. As these garments are meant only for cast, crew, producer and director, comparatively few are printed (around 100 for an average production) and they quickly become collectors' items; the more prestigious the programme, the higher their rating. Regularly swopping teeshirts with the loved one is the equivalent of the American fraternity habit of 'pinning',

The tribal hunting ground

How DID you guess?

There are various ways by which the keen student of *homo televisionis* can spot the burgeoning affair. One is when the same two people find themselves 'by chance' at the same table in the studio canteen every single day, a stage which is followed by studiously sitting apart. You can also often tell who is having an affair with whom by observing bar behaviour, especially after the programme in which all concerned have been working has just finished.

Another giveaway phrase is the innocuous-sounding 'Why don't we share a taxi?' Some TV centres conveniently have boards or taxi sheets so that you can monitor who's leaving together; indeed, as most studios are in out of the way places involving constant stream of taxis from studio to home residence, anyone who could get hold of a week's taxi sheets could construct a whole amatory network.

And anyone wearing the teeshirt (qv) of a programme he or she is not involved in suggests a favour has been exchanged somewhere along the line.

while many a secret affair has come to light when a pretty young thing with no power or influence walks in wearing one that's particularly scarce. Sexual bribery is considered a small price for the delicious ego trip of being the first to walk into your own studio wearing this glittering prize.

The Pleasure Dome

In the unpromising setting of the BBC Rehearsal Centre – an eight-storey tower block in West London off the M4 – lies the jewel in the Corporation's Crown. As a happy hunting-ground for potential lovers, its top-floor restaurant is a *nonpareil*. Here at any one time are gathered the personnel from about ten different shows – actors, producers, secretaries, executives, assistants. Once inside this vast room, amid the constant welter of hugging, kissing, appraising glances and cries of 'Darling! So you're going to be here for six weeks, then!' new alliances are formed and current relationships become apparent. As there is no booking and seating is supposedly random, who sits with whom on subsequent days is highly significant. In the opinion of many experts, there is no finer or more efficient dating centre in the western world.

CRUMPLING THE DUVET

– BBC argot for making love

(Attributed to the legendary Professor Laurie Taylor, who once answered the telephone out of breath with the words 'I was just uncrumpling the duvet')

12 Love in Publishing

GREAT EXPECTATIONS

PERSUASION

UTOPIA

WAR AND PEACE

DECLINE AND FALL

REMEMBRANCE
OF THINGS PAST

It is not going too far to say that without its highly incestuous love life, British publishing would fall to pieces. Editors who have affairs with agents learn about a future bestseller while it is still merely a twinkle in some accountant's eye, rights buyers get the inside track for the paperback everyone's bidding for in the same way, glossy lady authors seduce male publishers into paying hefty advances for a book that finally has to be written by some hard-working ghost hired for a couple of thousand (look for the phrase 'editorial collaboration'), while good reviews for some fairly pointless book can literally be screwed out of certain literary journalists. And everyone tries to put the make on publicity girls.

One reason for all this breathless activity is that publishing contains a disproportionate number of single people. Especially women: because of the low rates of pay, most second-tier staff are female, so every publishing house has its corps of dedicated editorial women, single, divorced or – like resting actresses – between relationships, who are the profession's backbone. The ghetto effect of the low pay which stops them looking outward for entertainment is aggravated by long hours, an extraordinarily high level of commitment, and drink. For

most of publishing, from the regular in-house, after-hours socialising to the hype-hype-hooray of launch parties, is fuelled by a veritable sea of alcohol.

Because they so outnumber men, often the first moves towards embroilment are made by women, especially if their jobs involve inviting authors, agents or journalists out to lunch (expense accounts are another key factor in the romantic life of the publishing world); and many an unwary literary editor has discovered too late that there is no such thing as a free lunch. As for colleagues, 'They're shutting up the office – why don't we go on discussing this over a glass of wine?' has launched a thousand slips.

Publishing affairs fall into the usual two categories, in-house or external (which means in someone else's publishing office).

In-house affairs are characterised by two salient points: the first is that despite the fact that the average publishing office resembles a rabbit warren on six floors, everyone knows about them from the word go; and the second is that if there is any kind of trouble one of you has to leave (and she doesn't always go quietly). Certain houses are much more shirty about the in-house affair than others, which almost always means that the Managing Director is a Lothario who can't keep his hands off the secretaries. Only when these leave with such frequency that he finds himself short of staff does he turn his attention to an external, usually settling on someone useful, like the features editor of a magazine who can be guaranteed to give good reviews or buy extracts.

The ending of the in-house affair is often messy, especially in the old-style publisher's office. This is generally a tall, narrow, elegant Georgian house, which the junior staff (who are crammed into small, badly lit rooms and who have to share one loo that doesn't flush properly) hate because it is cold, draughty and awkward. The senior executives, installed in the grand first-floor reception rooms that are too big to partition, adore their working surroundings and enjoy impressing visitors with the gracious charm exuded by the walls of the ancient building. The thick carpet with which the floors are invariably covered to prevent the dust of centuries rising has meant that all too frequently an editor and his secretary fail to

❝ The hype-hype hooray of launch parties is fuelled by a veritable sea of alcohol ❞

hear the art director's footsteps and are caught locked in each other's arms; the stairs mean that after the final, agonised farewell or the unexpected jilting, you pass your ex-love five times daily on the way to Production in the basement. For like the trolls in the Black Forest, those who do the real work in publishing usually live underground.

Where it all happens

Because of the number of people in publishing single for one reason or another, it is very seldom that both parties in an affair happen to be married at any given moment. This means that romantic fulfilment can usually take place on the home territory of one of them; it is only when a senior publisher, with a high salary, personal income or plenty of the firm's money at his disposal, jibs at going back to the Clapham bedsitting room of the new publicity assistant in her lunch hour, that the hotel trade makes a profit.

Fortunately, one aspect of the gentlemanliness that all publishers fondly believe characterises every last action of the profession is the readiness to lend a flat to a friend (with the constantly-changing pattern of both jobs and lovers, who knows when you too might be in need of this friendly service?). Leaving a bottle of drink as a thank you is considered chic. One sign of the borrower is a bulging briefcase or a muttered excuse about calling in at the laundry on the way home, ('it's the only time it's open'). In both cases, the difficulty of concealing a pair of sheets that are first clean, then crumpled, is the reason.

Even with the utmost precautions, though, these secret assignations have a way of becoming known to a wider audience. Publishing has observers everywhere. 'When I was having an affair with a paperback editor' says one rights director, 'a col-

league with a flat on the second floor of an old building loaned him the key. When we pressed the front door buzzer I realised the girl who opened it was the sister of one of my authors, who I'd met at his dinner party. We were very civilised and didn't recognise each other, but upstairs I laughed so much I could hardly do what we'd gone there for.' Only after comparative calm had set in was she able to enjoy her Penguin.

Who to have an affair with

Affairs in publishing are to the individual rather as feathers on the side are to an arrow – highly visible, adding interest to the basic profile and, above all, capable of guiding and directing progress.

With this in mind, it is obvious that the only suitable object for lust or love is someone creative (i.e., commissions creative work from others, writes about it, or more rarely, produces it); or who has access to the firm's cheque book. Best of all cachetwise are those who combine both: the publisher who is also a commissioning editor, or the rights director with a flair for finding notable paperbacks.

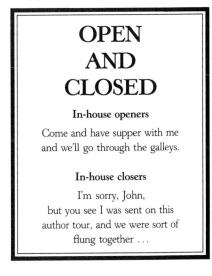

OPEN AND CLOSED

In-house openers

Come and have supper with me
and we'll go through the galleys.

In-house closers

I'm sorry, John,
but you see I was sent on this
author tour, and we were sort of
flung together . . .

The truly creative publishing affair is so constructive in terms of image that many people, who in other fields would marry, prefer to allow their respective divorces to slip past unnoticed in the general tribute to the Sartre/de Beauvoir school of romantic literary bohemianism. Publishing is sprinkled with long-term liaisons between literary editors of serious newspapers and heads of Non-Fiction Departments, rights directors and commissioning editors.

Shorter affairs tend to be more explosive. Publishing houses have been all but brought to their knees when some entirely unsuitable person has been brought in to a top job through the intrigues of their lover – or by the fallout when the affair ends, which often results in the exodus of one or more directors ('I'm going to form my own imprint') along with a clutch of junior staff. Sometimes there is revenge: when one woman publisher was having an affair with the academic from whom she had commissioned a book, the scheduled print run was an unprecedented (for him) print run of 10,000. When the affair finished just after completion of the manuscript, she cut it to 5,000, and put back the publication date.

The Publisher

The cherished self-image tucked away inside The Publisher's head, often in the teeth of evidence to the contrary, is that of a gentleman. A second son, maybe – is not the world of books the *intellectual* alternative to the Church? – this scholarly figure, in his well-cut classic clothes that have seen better days, has a breadth of mind that expands to visionary concepts of a better, brighter world, particularly over a good lunch (this is the only point at which the dream invariably coincides sharply with reality). Generous to a fault with his authors, his only wish is to see the written word accorded the respect it deserves and his ancient publishing house serve the noble purpose of nurturing talented fledglings.

While it is perfectly true that many gentlemen in that sense do remain in publishing, their numbers are dwindling. Just as the grey squirrel drove out the native red by every means short of actual physical assault, so the new breed is forcing out the old; gone are the old, happy days where not making very much money was the hallmark of respectability in a hardback publisher – the grey squirrels are swapping ten per cent discounts for 60 days' free credit with booksellers, watching the flow chart, or forgetting books altogether and plunging into software. And having affairs.

Sometimes an affair with a senior staff member and the wealth of information gathered thereby is the means by which a new-style publisher arrives in a traditional

---

OPENING GAMBITS
from publisher to author

- Why don't you come round to my place and we can discuss the contract in more detail?
- I think we'd better go over your synopsis together – how about next Tuesday?
- There are one or two points I'm not happy about in Chapter Four – how about next Tuesday?
- What about coming to the Sunday Times party with me?
- Would you like a guiding hand on your Author Tour?
- We ought to discuss your next book some time – how about next Tuesday?
- If you need somewhere to work quietly, I've got this little cottage in the country . . .
- I think we ought to make it dinner – I always believe in discussing fiction over a glass of wine.
- Of *course* I'll show you how to work a word processor. As it happens, I've got one myself – how about coming round next Tuesday?
- Of course I'll show you my word processor. Actually, I do all my writing in the bedroom.

hardback house, to land there with a clash of styles audible all round Bedford Square. In these cases, everyone waits to see what will happen once the affair is over. For if there are rows and jealousies, one party generally leaves; invariably, irrespective of age, seniority and standing in the company or even the rights and wrongs of the case, this is the woman (one of the unwritten rules of publishing is 'The Woman always goes').

Sometimes she gets her revenge by becoming a rights director and offering ludicrously small sums for her ex-lover's new novel (many publishers fancy themselves as writers on the side) before withdrawing from the deal at the last minute because 'I can't persuade *anybody* that it'll sell'. This technique is known to publishers as *contractus interruptus*.

The length and flammability quotient of these liaisons is also affected by whether the publisher involved is hardback (Arts or

❝ Mr Priestley, I really do think we should stop ❞

English degree, *cares* about literature) or paperback. Paperback publishers, who wear dark glasses where other publishers wear spectacles, are trendy, downmarket, cash-oriented and raffish; like their books, they may be easy to pick up and compulsively readable – but you don't always want to give them shelf-room.

Authors

The relationship between an author and his or her publisher and editor is pregnant – and I use the word advisedly – with romantic possibilities. Lady authors are frequently courted by publishers who woo them with anything from dinner at the Ritz and trips to New York to mammoth advances in every sense of the word plus someone actually to write the book. Some publishers find it difficult to believe that their own personal charms are not sufficient inducement to tumble into their arms; if rejected, they snatch back the bottle of half-finished supermarket plonk with the words 'no sense in wasting this' and exit towards a more likely prospect.

Sometimes the boot is on the other foot. J. B. Priestley was famous in publishing circles for running round a boardroom table after a female editor twice his size and of minimal looks. 'Mr Priestley, I really do think we should stop' she would pant as she tried to dodge for the door; today, certain male authors have a name for pouncing.

One of the Pan stable is notorious for always trying it on, and there are several on the Cape list who believe that the phrase 'author's rights' extends to the bodies of the staff as well as royalties. Many regard the Publicity Department, in particular, as there to serve them in every way, hence the feeling that they have a kind of *droit de seigneur* over the Publicity girls, who are usually young, pretty and well-educated (see below).

Others authors need pampering and mollycoddling to make them feel sufficiently loved and wanted to produce a weekly chapter, sulking like a child if their editor forgets the daily 'And how is your cold this morning?' call. On the whole, though women can be prima donnas, it is the men who develop an ego as big as the Ritz, often starting up an affair with their editor as a means of securing more favourable treatment than her other authors get, if not her whole attention. As such personalities are often hidden behind lean, handsome and hungry masks, the harassed editor frequently falls headlong into the author's arms; only if her publishing house succeeds in holding him to the option on his next book does the affair continue.

The Literary Agent

The best agents are like the nosecones on a guided missile, unerringly seeking out the heat in the form of the most suitable publisher and the largest advance. They are also razor sharp, able to spot the small print in a contract at a distance of a hundred yards through a thick fog, and gifted with the knack of working out the difference in a $7\frac{1}{2}$ per cent and a 10 per cent royalty on sales of 25,000 at £8.95 in dollars and yen simultaneously before so much as opening their mouths.

All writers should have agents because publishers, under the guise of protecting the writer from the brutal world of hard commercial fact, and with their natural predilection for the status quo, will keep him on the same financial level for years ('this is our standard contract, and because it's you, I'm putting in an option'); whereas the agent's first rule of thumb is that every contract should be better than the one it succeeds.

Many agents have an extraordinary high level of libido but on the whole the authors they represent are sancrosanct, the agents confining their attentions to rights directors, commissioning editors, paperback publishers and other agents, but seldom publicity girls – no sense in distracting them from the agent's authors.

When two agents have an affair together, the aftermath can range from bitter competitiveness to a reminiscent but uneasy gleam in the eye ('He/she knows all my negotiating tricks and my authors' advances') if the affair fails to gell or comes apart. If it's True Love, however, there could be something all agents hope for: a new and powerful partnership, boths sides pooling their lists, dovetailing their specialities, splitting the cost of staff and premises. And – now that they can represent The Author so much more fully – jacking up their percentages.

The Publicity Girl

Like selling rights or being an editor, publicity is a traditionally female area. Publicity departments used to be staffed by bright ex-secretaries who picked up whatever a hard-pressed executive was willing to delegate. As booking hotels and arranging provincial radio interviews for an author with as much charisma as a field mouse came low on the executive's list of priorities, Shirley from Chigwell soon found herself known as *Our Publicity Girl*.

Today's publicity girl is a bright young graduate in her twenties with a degree in English from Exeter, Oxford or, more rarely, Cambridge – the whole of publishing is gradually becoming better educated, thanks to the competition for employment. All of them help each other get new jobs at regular intervals (all publishing houses have an inbuilt resistance to the idea of the pay rise, so job-swapping is generally the way to more money), meet at parties like those given by the Publishers' Publicity Circle, know exactly who is doing what with whom but never, ever badmouth each other.

Because publicity girls have got to be friendly and available, everyone makes

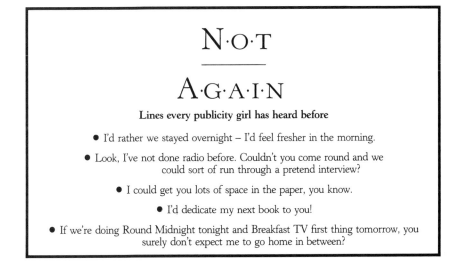

N·O·T

A·G·A·I·N

Lines every publicity girl has heard before

- I'd rather we stayed overnight – I'd feel fresher in the morning.
- Look, I've not done radio before. Couldn't you come round and we could sort of run through a pretend interview?
- I could get you lots of space in the paper, you know.
- I'd dedicate my next book to you!
- If we're doing Round Midnight tonight and Breakfast TV first thing tomorrow, you surely don't expect me to go home in between?

passes at them, from the authors they take on tour to gossip column journalists and literary editors, many of whom are lonely men whose marriages are either over or without much meaning. Nobody warns the publicity girl which author, editor or journalist has an appalling track record, so her life is full of surprises, with one of her greatest problems how to keep on the friendly terms essential to her job with someone she has had to rebuff decisively.

The Publishing Lunch

The Publishing Lunch is not so much a way of keeping body and soul together between the snatched breakfast – because of the low pay, publishing people tend to live in the remoter postal districts – and the post-pub dinner, as part of publishing ethos, not to say mystique. The primary purpose can be business meeting, self-advertisement, sales conference, launching pad for liaisons, opportunity for some serious drinking, or general break for enjoyment in the middle of the day. In publishing, *everybody* lunches, hence the saying at the rougher end of the trade: 'I've had more hot dinners than you've had affairs'. Quite often this is true.

Lunching takes place in circumstances as blatantly public as possible. The preferred number is two, and voyeurism is not only permitted but encouraged – the more people who see you lunch, the better pleased both of you are.

Who lunches? Hardback publishers lunch paperback rights representatives, newspapers lunch paperback publicity departments, commissioning editors lunch

'Actually, I see it as a BIG book ...'

> **All-purpose opening gambit
> for arranging a lunch**
>
> - I wonder if you'd have a look at this
>   book and tell me what you think?
>
> **All-purpose excuse for breaking a lunch date**
>
> - Terribly sorry, but I've got to go down
>   and see the printer.

authors, hardback publicity girls lunch newspaper columnists or magazine features editors. Publishers lunch everyone: agents, authors and – if they want to send a nervous *frisson* round both their houses at the thought of possible merger – each other. Agents who have to pay out of their own pockets rather than slap the bill on the firm's account, tend to lunch with a direct purpose in mind – persuading a magazine, say, that second rights will still seem new and fresh to the readers after the Daily Mail have creamed off the first ('there's plenty for *everyone* in this book').

And where? Covent Garden has taken over from Soho as the main area, though traditionalists still prefer places like *Chez Gerard* in Charlotte Street and *L'Escargot,* whose round central tables are ideal for holding court. Also in Charlotte Street is *Rue St Jacques;* people from Granadaland often go to the *Gay Hussar* because of Victor's amazing welcome and the enormous helpings (though the penalty is one is often seated opposite Lord Longford). The *Savoy* is avoided because it is always full of journalists (see Fleet Street) who might overhear what they are not meant to hear, but the *Connaught* is All Right. Publishers who lunch at the Ritz are often suspect financially as well as other ways. In Covent Garden you cannot throw a stuffed olive without hitting some publisher in the eye: to catch up on the latest publishing coups, visit Bertorelli's in Floral Street, *Magno's Brasserie, Mon Plaisir, Bianchi's, Luigi's,* and

Joe Allen's for a widescreen view. *Le Porte de la Cité* is the nearest to Sphere; Collins people can get anywhere in W.1, *Hilaire* in the Old Brompton Road is a Penguin hangout and the whole of Pan go to *11 Park Walk.* Hardback publishers with large expense accounts go to *Interlude de Tabaillau* or the *Neal Street Restaurant;* paperback ones go to *Langan's,* especially if they are lunching a Name. 'Our Contracts Department will be in touch with you' is Publishing for 'Goodbye'.

The Party

Publishing life is punctuated with parties and everyone goes, because publishing is a highly social industry and visibility is a key

HOW PUBLISHERS ANNOUNCE AN ENGAGEMENT
Extract from Publishing News, Friday April 26, 1985

There is more Dallas-style drama at Century-Hutchinson. The story of money and power is now enhanced by the missing ingredient – love.

Dallas Manderson, Century-Hutchinson's Sales Director, is forging his owner merger by becoming engaged to Emma Hogan, a commissioning editor with the Stanley Paul imprint.

'We met at a party for Hutchinson' said Manderson. 'It's all happened within the last six weeks.'

The marriage will have to wait until Hogan's divorce is finalised. 'But I don't think this will be a problem', said Manderson. 'Emma's husband is a solicitor, and he's handling it. It's all very amicable.'

of-civilisation-as-we-know-it atmosphere, highly conducive to the abandonment of all normal restraint.

But the publishing party par excellence is the Book Party. You can tell roughly how much the publishers hope to make out of any one book by the number of staff there from the host firm (apart, that is, from Production and Sales, the rule being that those who have to roll up their sleeves, actually pick up boxes of books or otherwise get their hands dirty stay out of sight).

A big and splashy launch is like some enormous dating introduction service, with people in every corner furiously scribbling

Note the hand at the collar in the classic gesture of uncertainty. This man is about to come out with the current publishing euphemism for being unemployed: 'I'm planning a best-seller'.

factor in judging people's current success rate. If you haven't been mentioned in the trade news recently for a major deal, going to a party is one way of plugging this gap and stifling the cry of 'Whatever became of so and so?' (Best way of hiding the fact you haven't been asked is the response: 'I'm on the wagon'.) So the party is often the place where it all starts.

At the Christmas Party – huge, drunken and rather fun, with everyone out to dinner afterwards in huge groups at the same publishing restaurant where they all had lunch – there are plenty of excuses for the Chairman to lead the Senior Commissioning Editor down to Production in the basement to discuss plans for next year's blockbuster in the requisite privacy. At parties to celebrate being in the business five years without being taken over or going broke there are plenty of excuses for chatting up anyone else in the firm that you fancy; and at bankruptcy parties – one New York publisher sold tickets to his and used the money to pay his freelances – there is a general end-

telephone numbers and lunch dates in Filo-faxes. The air is loud with cries of 'So you're moving to Kensington too! We *must* have a drink!' as agents, reviewers, journalists, buyers from Hatchards and Selfridges, anx-ious-looking Rights people, assess the book's prospects and each other. The only person there who knows no one is the author, who can frequently be spotted alone and wretched in a corner while the party roars merrily along around him; and although only three people – author, editor and publicist – will actually have read the book, every single copy laid out will have disappeared by the end of the evening – often, like the guests, two at a time.

Book Fairs

But everything pales into insignificance beside the frenzied sexual carousels which masquerade as Book Fairs. Here, far from home, loved ones, the watching eyes of the rest of the office, and subsidised by the best the Accounts Department can offer, an atmosphere of misrule reigns, together with a tacit understanding that nobody will split

on anyone else when they all get home again. The opposite, and equally valid, point of view is that Frankfurt is full of frust-rated people, all suffering from that most common of sexual delusions – somewhere out there is a world full of adventure, being enjoyed by everyone except themselves.

Many publishers signal their carnival intentions from the word *Auf*. Some even change their clothes styles when on one of these jaunts – one man, famous for his well-cut suits at home, switches when abroad to jeans and threadbare jerseys, going to great trouble to get the holes in the right places. It is commonplace to be introduced by an unsuspecting colleague to the person you have just spent the night with, or to be woken by the noise down the passage of some importunate publisher hammering on the door of his new secretary. ('Let me in or I'll fire you!' is the warcry of one.)

Often the liaisons begun in Bologna or New York result in intercontinental job shifts, with rich lady rights managers from American publishers like Simon & Schuster or Random House crossing the Atlantic to a job in Bedford Square to be near their loved one, dropping in the process up to half their salary.

Not surprisingly, publishing people date their year by Book Fairs. 'She finally mar-ried him the week before Frankfurt' they say. The only Book Fair unpopular with British publishers is the London Book Fair, not because it takes place in the dreaded Barbican, but because few British publishers can bear to watch, as one put it, 'Those lucky foreigners doing what we'd be doing in Frankfurt while we just work hard and sell books.'

Yet in many ways liaisons at a Book Fair are rather like the books promoted there. 'You get madly enthusiastic about them when you're there and being carried away by the excitement of the atmosphere. But once you land at Heathrow, you forget them immediately.'

Photograph Credits

The author and publishers are grateful to the following for permission to reproduce their photographs:

pages 10 Dafydd Jones; 12 Patrick Ward; 13 Dafydd Jones; 16 Homer Sykes; 18 Rex Features Ltd; 19 Dafydd Jones; 25 Rex Features Ltd; 27 Sally and Richard Greenhill; 28, 33, 35 Dafydd Jones; 36 Rex Features Ltd; 38, 40, 41, 42, 43, 45 Bladon Lines Travel Ltd; 46, 49 Ambrose Greenway; 50 Laurie Sparham/Network; 54 Dafydd Jones; 56 Camera Press; 61 Desmond O'Neill Features; 62 Dafydd Jones; 66 Norman Potter/Rex Features Ltd; 68 London Express News and Features; 70 Champneys at Tring Health Resort; 73 Mike Abrahams/Network; 75 Sally and Richard Greenhill; 78 Dafydd Jones; 81 Homer Sykes; 83 Dafydd Jones; 89 Rex Features Ltd; 91 top London Express News and Features; 91 bottom Rex Features Ltd; 99 Thames Television; 103 London Express News and Features; 107 Richard Young/Rex Features Ltd; 109 BBC Hulton Picture Library; 111, 115 BPCC/Aldus Archive/Shaun Skelly; 121 Publishing News; 124 Mike Abrahams/Network; 126 Publishing News/Tessa Musgrave.